Dynamic Decision Support for Electronic Requirements Negotiations

Annika Lenz

Dynamic Decision Support for Electronic Requirements Negotiations

With a Foreword by Professor Mareike Schoop, PhD

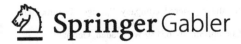

Annika Lenz
Information Systems Department 1
University of Hohenheim
Stuttgart-Hohenheim, Germany

Dissertation, University of Hohenheim 2019

D100

ISBN 978-3-658-31174-2   ISBN 978-3-658-31175-9   (eBook)
https://doi.org/10.1007/978-3-658-31175-9

This Springer Gabler imprint is published by the registered company Springer Fachmedien
Wiesbaden GmbH part of Springer Nature.
The registered company address is: Abraham-Lincoln-Str. 46, 65189 Wiesbaden, Germany

Foreword

Software development involves a variety of stakeholders who all have different goals and constraints during the development process. Consequently, they have different requirements regarding the software, the development process, the usability, the visualisation, the warranty etc. To come to an agreement, these requirements need to be discussed and aligned, i.e. they need to be negotiated. Such negotiations are called requirements negotiations.

Requirements negotiations are often conducted electronically. Electronic requirements negotiations are performed and supported by means of information and communication technology in terms of communication support, decision support, and/ or document management for the various stakeholders involved in a software development process. Such support is only possible through the adoption of information and communication technology which consequently offers additional value. The negotiation partners have various roles and need to deal with incomplete or missing information. Therefore, specific decision support is required enabling negotiators to make suitable (counter-)offers and to choose between alternatives.

Although decision support exists in various formats in digital negotiation systems, the challenge that electronic requirements negotiations pose is for decisions with incomplete or missing information to be supported. Such dynamic decision support does not yet exist other than by repeating the complete preference elicitation process to start afresh. Consequently, the research goal of the current book is to enable dynamic decision support for electronic requirements negotiations.

Existing decision support methods were assessed and compared and one was chosen to be extended allowing for the dynamics of changing preferences during an electronic requirements negotiation process. The new method was implemented and integrated into the negotiation support system Negoisst. Extensive evaluations show its merits compared to existing decision support methods.

The present work has important contributions for negotiation science as well as for decision science. A dynamic decision support method is presented that can be applied to environments in which preferences can change and decision support is required for a current decision problem with up-to-date preference information. The method is applicable to electronic negotiations in general and is not restricted to requirements negotiations. Practitioners will find a decision support tool in a negotiation support system to help them make the best possible decision in given circumstances.

The book reports on highly relevant research and deserves wide-spread dissemination.

Professor Mareike Schoop, PhD

Preface

This doctoral thesis was written during my work as a research assistant at the Information Systems Department I at the University of Hohenheim. I would like to take this opportunity to thank the numerous people who supported me in many ways, as well as those who accompanied me during my doctoral studies.

My greatest thanks go to Prof. Mareike Schoop, PhD for the excellent supervision and the enormous support during the entire time. She sparked my interest in research, always supported me and gave me the opportunity to present and discuss my research at international conferences. Furthermore, I would like to thank Prof. Dr. Markus Voeth for co-supervising my thesis, Prof. Dr. Katja Schimmelpfeng for chairing the board of examiners, and Prof. Dr. Herzwurm for the chance of working in the joint research project of the University of Stuttgart and the University of Hohenheim on electronic requirements negotiations and his full support during my time at his department.

I would also like to express my gratitude to my fellow colleagues at the Information Systems Department I at the University of Hohenheim Corina Blum, Simon Bumiller, Prof. Dr. Marc Fernandes, Dr. Johannes Gettinger, Muhammed Kaya, Dr. Michael Körner, Dr. Philipp Melzer, Andreas Schmid, and Dr. Bernd Schneider, whose regular discussions and fruitful conversations on a professional and personal level have always been a great help for me and positively influenced me. I thank the development team, who always gave their full commitment to the implementation of Negoisst.

Moreover, I would like to thank my former colleagues at the Information Systems Department II at the University of Stuttgart Christopher Jud, Dr. Benedikt Krams, Prof. Dr. Martin Mikusz, Dr. Norman Pelzl, Tobias Schäfer, Sook Ja Schmitz, Dr. Sixten Schockert, Tim Taraba, and Dr. Tobias Tauterat, whose intense discussions helped me especially in the beginning of my PhD project.

I gratefully acknowledge the financial support from the State Baden-Württemberg towards my PhD scholarship (Promotionsstipendium nach dem Landesgraduiertenförderungsgesetz, LGFG) and the funding received from the Federal Ministry of Education and Research (01PL16003) for the project Humboldt reloaded at the University of Hohenheim.

I thank my parents and brothers for their encouragement and their support during the work on this dissertation. Special thanks again go to my husband Philipp for his advice, suggestions, and thoughts throughout my PhD project, but also for his full support, loving words, and motivation.

Stuttgart-Hohenheim,   Annika Lenz

Table of Contents

List of Figures

List of Tables

List of Abbreviations

ARN	In agile requirements negotiation
ACA	Adaptive Conjoint Analysis
AHP	Analytic Hierarchy Process
ASE	Adaptive Self-Explication
AVE	Average variance extracted
AVG	Average
CA	Conjoint analysis
CARDS	Conjoint Adaptive Ranking Database
DynaDeS	Dynamic Decision Support
DynASE	Dynamic Adaptive Self-Explication
FastPACE	Fast Polyhedral Adaptive Conjoint Estimation
Hy	Hybrid
IEEE	Institute of Electrical and Electronics Engineers
KMO	Kaiser-Meyer-Olkin
M	Mean
Mdn	Median
MPSOE	Maximum possible sum of interpolation errors
GDP	General decision problem structure in negotiations
PASE	Presorted Adaptive Self-Explicated Approach
PCA	Principal component analysis
PCPM	Paired Comparison-based Preference Measurement
Req	Requirement
SD	Standard deviation
SE	Self-Explicated
TRN	In traditional requirements negotiation
TOPSIS	Technique for Order Preference by Similarity to Ideal Solution

1 Introduction

In software development, a vast array of requirements by diverse stakeholders (e.g. customers, architects, engineers, product managers, team leaders, developers, testers, future users, and maintainers) has to be taken into account (Fricker and Grünbacher 2008; Grünbacher and Seyff 2005). In the phase of requirements engineering, requirements are elicited, agreed upon, and specified (Sommerville 2012). Heterogeneous stakeholders desire different goals for the software to be developed (Boehm and Kitapci 2006; Grünbacher and Seyff 2005), therefore not all of their requirements can be implemented due to limited budget or limited time. Thus, there is a high risk of conflict about software requirements (Grünbacher and Seyff 2005). Although each of the stakeholders has individual preferences and objectives (Pohl 2010; Price and Cybulski 2006), they seek to reach the same overall goal of a software development product. They cannot reach this unilaterally, due to the fact that their tasks are interdependent (Lenz et al. 2015). To resolve their conflicts and come to a joint agreement concerning the requirements to be implemented or declined, involved stakeholders must share their information, ideas, and thoughts and exchange their arguments, which is done in the process of requirements negotiation (Lenz et al. 2015). Thus, requirements negotiation is a cooperative process of communication and decision making between all involved stakeholders with the objective of reaching an agreement about the software development process and outcome (Grünbacher and Seyff 2005; Herzwurm et al. 2012; Lenz et al. 2015). Requirements negotiation is an iterative and incremental process, in which the stakeholders' interaction is essential throughout the process to shape, specify, and agree upon requirements (Lenz et al. 2015; Pohl 2010; Reiser et al. 2012). Since these requirements are not completely specified in the beginning of the negotiation, they have to be developed throughout the process. Requirements negotiation must deal with incomplete or missing information. The information is subject to change during the process (Lenz et al. 2015). Although the stakeholders must decide on a joint agreement, they individually seek a compromise, in order to achieve the best outcome concerning their individual goals. Thus, one of their individual core activities is to compare offers with their negotiation partners' counteroffers (Gettinger and Koeszegi 2014). To help stakeholders focus on their interests and act accordingly, decision support has been proposed (cf. Raiffa et al. 2002; Vetschera 2006). However, to respond to and adequately address the uncertain and changing information during requirements negotiations, flexible decision support processes are needed to facilitate insertion, modification, or deletion of requirements (Grünbacher et al. 2006; Lenz et al. 2015).

A. Lenz, *Dynamic Decision Support for Electronic Requirements Negotiations*, https://doi.org/10.1007/978-3-658-31175-9_1

1.1 The Need for Dynamic Decision Support in Electronic Requirements Negotiations

Software development is characterised by its dynamic nature (Hansen et al. 2015; Jarke and Lyytinen 2015). Changes during the requirements negotiation process are very likely (Hull et al. 2011). These changes concern the changes of scope, delivery schedule, requirements, implementations, or preferences (Boehm and Kitapci 2006; Grünbacher and Seyff 2005). If these changes are not passed on to the decision support, decisions are made not reflecting the intended goals. If stakeholders try to achieve unaligned goals for requirements and their implementation, the negotiation outcome is influenced negatively (Raiffa et al. 2002).

Having up-to-date information is absolutely essential. Incorrect preference information not relating to the stakeholder's interests, jeopardises the benefits of decision support. Thus, the volatility of the requirements and their implementation alternatives throughout the project requires reassessment after obtaining new information. Although requirements are traceable in requirements management systems in theory, reassessment is a complex decision making process, which requires high cognitive load (Reiser et al. 2012; Simon 1955).

Multi-criteria decision aiding methods for preference elicitation must be adopted to the negotiation context to comprehensively fulfil the application domain's demands (Almeida and Wachowicz 2017). These methods originate from marketing research and thus are designed as one-shot approaches. They are not intended to adjust the measurement in retrospective, since this is not required for usage scenarios in marketing research. Accurate preferences are of great importance to support decisions meaningfully. This provides benefits especially in the phase of the actual negotiation and post-settlement. Therefore the timeliness of the preferences is of high priority to be able to carry out accurate negotiation analysis. However the dynamic perspective for electronic requirements negotiations is missing in existing approaches. Applying previous decision support research in negotiations to the domain of requirements negotiations and extending it by a dynamic perspective improves these approaches substantially.

Dynamic decision support takes the perspective of time into consideration. It considers unstable requirements, their implementation options, and their preferences by adjusting the decision making basis. Dynamic decision support is supposed to facilitate the adjustment without having to actively reassess existing requirements. Flexible processes are needed that allow for preference adjustment in an efficient way, as well as adequate decision support that does not depend on a complete re-evaluation (Reiser et al. 2012).

1.2 Research Objective and Research Questions

The depicted gap addresses the need for decision support tasks during the preparation phase. Preference measurement is an indispensable task for providing decision support. The contribution of this doctoral thesis addresses the depicted gap by introducing dynamic decision support for requirements negotiations.

Hereby, an individual's perspective is taken, which means that the objective is to enable one actor to interactively elicit preferences and adjust their measurement during the negotiation phase according to an increasing knowledge about requirements and their implementation scenarios. Decision support then relies dynamically on these adjusted preferences. Thus, the objective of the present thesis is to enable efficient dynamic decision support in electronic requirements negotiations, which can therefore be divided into 1) identification of relevant decision problem structures in electronic requirements negotiations and selection of the most relevant one; 2) assessment of the state-of-the-art preference measurement methods to be applied respectively assessment of their potential to expand them for dynamic means; 3) design of a dynamic preference adjustment method building on the assessment; and 4) implementation of the method developed in electronic decision support for requirements negotiations and evaluation of the designed dynamic decision support component. In order to achieve this, the following research questions will be answered in this thesis.

Research question 1: Which factors determine the decision context in requirements negotiations?

To build the foundation for dynamic decision support, first, the contextual factors for decision making during requirements negotiations must be studied. Research question 1 aims to analyse the decision context in requirements negotiations. Therefore, it aims to 1) identify and analyse the decision problem structure in requirements negotiations, which must be supported; 2) identify the types of issues, which are negotiated; 3) analyse the dynamics in requirements negotiations identifying scenarios of preference changes, possibly induced by agenda changes. The decision problem structure is addressed in chapter 3, the scenarios are identified in chapter 4, whilst chapters 5 and 6 build on the results.

Research question 2: How can an individual negotiator be supported best in his or her decisions in requirements negotiations?

Research question 2 addresses the design of dynamic decision support for requirements negotiations. It assesses state-of-the-art preference measurement methods referring to their suitability for dynamic scenarios and their potential to be expanded. The method with the most potential is expanded to fit dynamic demands, namely address the scenarios identified in research question 1. The decision support of the negotiation support system Negoisst (Schoop et al. 2003; Schoop 2010) is adapted to utilise the adjusted preferences.

The objective of dynamic decision support is to handle preference changes efficiently, which forms the main design goal for the component. For quality assurance, the preference measurement must result in accurate preferences as well as the decision makers' perception must correspond to the resulting preferences.

To reach this goal, state-of-the-art multi-criteria preference measurement approaches are assessed in terms of their performance and their suitability for a dynamic measurement. In order to achieve this, requirements for such dynamic preference measurement are derived, which are utilised to analyse the methods' potential to be expanded to enable dynamic preference adjustment (chapter 4).

Based on these findings, an extension is built to facilitate dynamic decision support, which enables dynamic preference adjustment during the negotiation process efficiently (chapter 5). Preference changes resulting from agenda changes (changes in the scope of the decision problem, i.e. addition, withdrawal, modification of issues and/or alternatives) or resulting from information increase without agenda changes are addressed.

Existing decision support for negotiations is adopted to incorporate the developed dynamic preference measurement method. The concept of such dynamic decision support (chapter 6) is implemented in a negotiation support system.

The designed dynamic decision support is evaluated by two means. First, the preference elicitation and adjustment processes are empirically evaluated by performance measures in laboratory experiments using a negotiation simulation (chapter 5.5). Second, the dynamic decision support component is evaluated in a scenario-based comparison with two state-of-the-art decision support components for requirements negotiations following a descriptive approach (chapter 6.5).

1.3   Structure of this Thesis

The structure of this cumulative doctoral thesis is depicted in Figure 1. The theoretical background and overall research methodology of this thesis are described in chapter two. Chapter three identifies relevant decision problems in requirements negotiations to be supported. It presents variants of the decision problem to focus on the most common decision problem structure. Chapter four builds on these findings, analysing preference measurement methods suitable for the identified problem structure. It analyses state-of-the-art preference measurement methods for their suitability and extension potential for dynamic demands. Chapter five expands the most suitable preference measurement method assessed in chapter four by a dynamic perspective. The newly developed dynamic method is integrated in a negotiation support system. Empirical studies are carried out to confirm the efficiency of the dynamic method developed. Chapter six evaluates the designed dynamic decision support in requirements negotiations against two alternative support components. Chapter seven concludes this thesis by summarising its contributions, discussing the findings with a critical acclaim, their limitations, and presenting implications for future research.

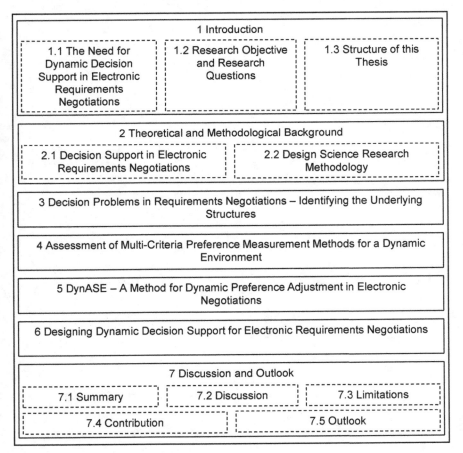

Figure 1: Structure of this thesis

2 Theoretical and Methodological Background

Requirements negotiation is a core activity in requirements engineering (Pohl 2010). Whilst negotiation research contributes to the research area by approaches to support negotiation processes, requirements engineering brings in the domain knowledge (Lenz et al. 2016). Chapter 2.1 focuses on an integrated perspective of both research areas to depict the state-of-the-art of decision support in electronic requirements negotiations. Chapter 2.2 describes the research approach to accomplish the objective of this thesis in the interdisciplinary domain of electronic requirements negotiations.

2.1 Decision Support in Electronic Requirements Negotiations

Raiffa et al. (2002) distinguish between two perspectives of decision making, which are both relevant in negotiation: individual decision making and plural decision making. Decision analysis, taking an individual perspective of decision making, focuses on a normative and prescriptive approach relevant for one individual actor or one negotiation party. Negotiation theory as a perspective of plural decision making presumes joint decision making. Negotiation theory is a predominantly prescriptive approach, which describes how real people could behave more beneficial in a collaborative decision. They are both integrated in asymmetric negotiation analysis, which is part of decision support in electronic negotiations. Asymmetric negotiation analysis attempts to support one's own position, considering the behaviour of the negotiating partner (Reiser 2013) and "advise[s] one party about how it should behave in order to achieve its best outcome" (Raiffa et al. 2002, p. 11). Hence, decision support integrates the two perspectives of decision making, taking an individual decision making view in a joint decision making context.

The prerequisite for such decision support is that the individual preferences of the negotiating parties are measured beforehand. There are three different groups of methods for this purpose, whose aim is to quantify the preferences in the form of a utility function. In the compositional preference measurement, preferences are directly elicited by the decision maker (e.g. self-explicated approaches, for an overview see Eckert and Schaaf 2009). These provide very quick and easy preference measurement, while the cognitive complexity for the decision maker is arguably low. By contrast, decompositional approaches (e.g. conjoint analysis, Green and Srinivasan 1990) measure the overall preference for an object with several attributes, from which partial utility values can be calculated. Since trade-off decisions are made here, real decision situations arise. This results in a higher cognitive load, especially as the number of attributes and attribute values increases. Hybrid methods try to combine the advantages of these groups, for example by first assessing the importance of the attributes and then performing conjoint tasks in which only the most important attributes are reassessed (Reiser 2013).

Information and communication technology provides benefit for these decision tasks (Schoop 2010). Electronic negotiation systems aim to support the three phases of a negotiation: the planning phase, the negotiation phase and the post-settlement phase. Negotiation support systems evolved from decision support systems (Lim and Benbasat 1992), which support the decision making process, help the decision makers to understand the problem and assess the implications of their decisions (French et al. 2009). Thus, negotiation support systems have an inherent characteristic of providing decision support. Facing multiple objectives in negotiations, decision support in negotiation support systems is most often based on multi-attribute utility theory (Keeney and Raiffa 1976). Multi-attribute utility theory enables defining utility functions for the decision makers based on their preferences for available alternatives. Current negotiation support systems use linear-additive utility functions (e.g. Kersten and Noronha 1999a; Schoop et al. 2003; Thiessen and Soberg 2003). A linear-additive utility model makes it possible to calculate the utility of a single offer, on the basis of the importance of the negotiation issues and the partial utility values of the negotiation values (alternatives). The partial utility values of single alternatives as well as the utility of specified offers form the basis for negotiation analysis (Raiffa et al. 2002).

Electronic requirements negotiations are carried out with and supported by information and communication technologies in the form of communication support, decision support and / or document management (Lenz et al. 2015). Existing approaches for electronic requirements negotiation serve different support objectives (cf. Lenz et al. 2016). Automated approaches autonomously perform requirements negotiations based on previously specified criteria (e.g. Mu et al. 2011; Zhang et al. 2013). For this purpose, individual preferences of the negotiating parties are collected prior to the actual negotiation process to enable the negotiation software to reveal conflicts between requirements. In the event of a conflict, autonomous software agents are used to resolve them according to the preferences disclosed.

The agile software development paradigm brings the customer needs and customer collaboration into focus, aims at shorter development cycles, and embraces change (Beck et al. 2001b). Consequently, activities in agile requirements engineering are addressed in each development cycle (Ramesh et al. 2010) in contrast to activities in traditional requirements engineering, which precede development. Thus, whilst negotiation in traditional requirements engineering focuses on resolving conflicts, negotiation in agile requirements engineering focuses more on refining requirements, changing and prioritising them in shorter iterations than negotiation in traditional requirements engineering does. (Ramesh et al. 2010)

The most widely used approach in the area of interactive requirements negotiation support is the EasyWinWin approach or variations of it (Boehm and Kitapci 2006; In and Olson 2004; Ruhe et al. 2002). They are based on Theory W (Boehm and Kitapci 2006), a project management approach aimed at achieving a fair agreement among all stakeholders involved by attempting to meet the win conditions of each stakeholder (Boehm and Kitapci 2006). Win conditions cover the stakeholders' needs, wishes, and/or requirements. The systems based on Theory W aim to support conflict resolution in the event of conflicts during requirements negotiation workshops by eliciting and disclosing stakeholder preferences.

2.2 Design Science Research Methodology

As the objective of this thesis is to design efficient dynamic decision support for requirements negotiations, the focus is set on a dynamic preference measurement method. To answer the research questions defined in section 1.2, the methodology applied is embedded in the design science research framework proposed by Hevner et al. (2004). Research question 1 aims to identify requirements for a dynamic preference measurement method. Based on these requirements, answering research question 2 dynamic preference measurement and dynamic decision support are designed in two design-cycles followed by an evaluation of the designed artefacts.

The selected research framework supports to reach the design-oriented goal of this thesis by "[...] address[ing] important unsolved problems in unique or innovative ways or solved problems in more effective or efficient ways" (Hevner et al. 2004, p. 81). In build and evaluate cycles, the artefact is iteratively developed and further improved. To conduct the design process in a rigorous way, general requirements for the class of electronic preference measurement in requirements negotiations are derived following explanatory design theory (Baskerville and Pries-Heje 2010). These cover the decision problem structure in requirements negotiations, types of requirements negotiation issues, change scenarios in requirements negotiations, and requirements for a dynamic preference

measurement method. To design a general solution, a general dynamic preference adjustment method (i.e. DynASE) and a general dynamic decision support
process (i.e. DynaDeS) are deduced. Thus, this work delivers the holistic concept
of DynaDeS incorporating DynASE and the instantiation of both as situated
implementations of the artefacts.

Gregor and Hevner (2013) provide a classification of the research contribution according to the application domain maturity and the solution maturity.
Since both the solution maturity (dynamic decision support process) and the
application domain maturity (electronic requirements negotiations) of this topic
are rather low, a two-cycle design is followed, in which artefacts in different
quadrants are developed. The first cycle applies routine design to build a proper
basis. The preference measurement method identified as the most suitable one is
applied for decision support in electronic negotiations. The second cycle contributes as improvement and exaptation leading to an innovation. As improvement, a
new solution (dynamic preference adjustment) is developed for the mature application domain of electronic negotiations. In the exaptation-quadrant, decision
support as known solution is extended to the immature domain of electronic
requirements negotiations. These two contributions are utilised to develop dynamic preference adjustment and dynamic decision support (new solution) in
electronic requirements negotiations (immature application domain), which
forms an innovation, see Figure 2.

Since this work aims to contribute in both rather low application domain
maturity and low solution maturity, two design alternatives are studied. For the
first alternative, the "static preference adjustment", the Adaptive Self-
Explication approach (ASE) by Netzer and Srinivasan (2011) is used, which is
an efficient approach for measuring an individual's preferences only once. Its
design is adapted in this thesis to be applied in a dynamic context by repeating its
preference elicitation steps. Consequently, the static alternative is less complex
and easier to implement but requires repetition of preference elicitation steps.
The second design alternative, DynASE, also builds on the ASE by utilising its
basic mechanisms and preference elicitation steps. However, it is developed to
avoid unnecessary repetition, which makes DynASE on the contrary a complex,
but efficient approach, since it manages to trace preference information.
DynaDeS is designed to incorporate both design alternatives.

This thesis applies the following research process to reach the goal of designing interactive dynamic decision support. Based on the general requirements
in the exploratory phase, a suitable method for preference measurement is chosen in the first conceptual phase, implemented in the instantiation phase, and
evaluated in a pre-study during the first confirmative phase. A second design and
evaluation cycle (Hevner 2007) enables to improve the method and its im-

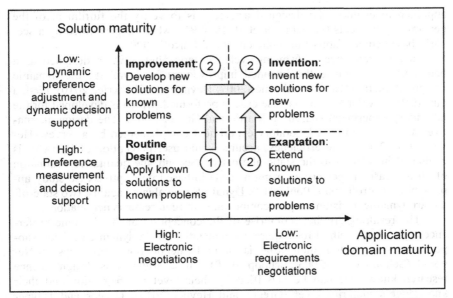

Figure 2:   Classification of research contribution (adapted from Gregor and Hevner 2013, p. 345)

plementation based on the results of the first confirmative phase. Furthermore, in the conceptual phase of the second cycle, the method is expanded to fit dynamic adjustment needs. In two evaluations, the dynamic preference adjustment arte-facts are evaluated.

The evaluation of the designed dynamic preference measurement method and the adapted dynamic decision support processes consequently comprises of a formative evaluation in the first cycle, and a summative evaluation in the second cycle (Venable et al. 2016). In the first cycle, a formative evaluation is chosen to demonstrate feasibility and identify potential for improvement. The focus lies on the assessment of the instantiation of the preference elicitation method and the decision support process. The preference elicitation cycle additionally seeks to enhance the artefacts by complementing the quantitative data qualitatively with the participants' remarks and suggestions for improvement. In the second cycle, a summative approach is chosen to evaluate the artefacts (Venable et al. 2016). Two types of evaluation are conducted in the preference adjustment cycle to ensure both the method's performance and the component's broader applicabil-ity. The focus of the evaluation lies on the novel component designed for the novel process of dynamic decision support in requirements negotiations. It co-vers the efficacy of the designed artefacts (Hevner et al. 2004). The adequate approach to evaluate the designed artefacts, is to verify the fulfilment of the general requirements (Nunamaker et al. 1990/91), which is performed by a scenario-based comparison of the component (cf. Carroll 2000).

In the preference adjustment cycle, a static alternative is designed as a benchmark to evaluate the intended improvement by DynASE, the dynamic design alternative (Gregor and Jones 2007; Hevner and Chatterjee 2010). First, a quantitative evaluation for one use case is performed, which is developed for the laboratory experiment (based on Martin and Gregor 2005). The design alternatives are evaluated by a laboratory experiment complemented by a survey (Hevner et al. 2004). The efficiency, accuracy, and user perception of DynASE is evaluated in relation to the static alternative. Second, the qualitative evaluation of all use cases is performed using a scenario-based descriptive case study approach (cf. Carroll 2000; Pohl 2010). DynaDeS is evaluated against two state-of-the-art dynamic decision support components for requirements negotiations.

The resulting artefacts comprise of the conception of the dynamic preference adjustment method for requirements negotiations, a dynamic decision support process, as well as their instantiation in the negotiation support system Negoisst (Schoop et al. 2003; Schoop 2010). These artefacts as design science research knowledge can be classified by their level of abstraction and their knowledge's maturity level (Gregor and Hevner 2013). Gregor and Hevner (2013) propose three maturity levels of design science research contribution types: Level 1 covers specific knowledge, e.g. instantiations of products or processes, while level 2 categorises more abstract and mature knowledge. Contributions at level 2 describe nascent design theory, which may cover design principles, models, or methods. At level 3, describing the most abstract, mature, and complete knowledge, design theories are developed. In this thesis, the instantiation of the static preference adjustment, the instantiation of DynASE, and the instantiation of DynaDeS represent situated implementations, which characterise them as artefacts on level 1. The conceptualisation of the static design alternative, DynASE, and DynaDeS describe more abstract knowledge, which contributes to knowledge as operational principles and architecture, and thus contribute as level 2 artefacts. Figure 3 shows the research process applied in this thesis.

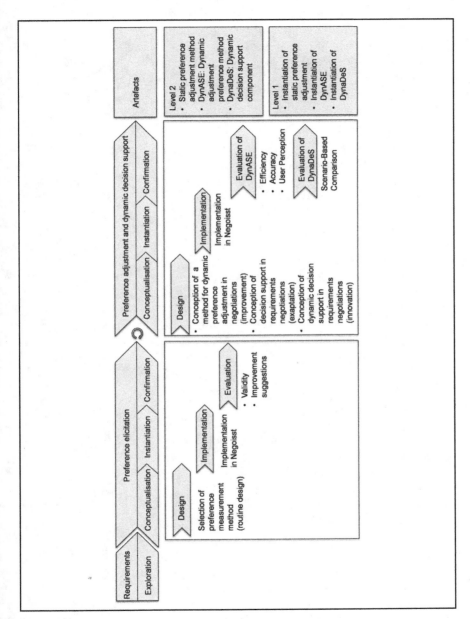

Figure 3:   Research process

3 Decision Problems in Requirements Negotiations[1]

3.1 Introduction

Requirements negotiations are iterative processes, in which involved parties with (usually conflicting) individual goals jointly seek to reach an overall goal, namely agreeing on a software development process and outcome (Lenz et al. 2015). One of their main characteristics is that involved parties need to make decisions during these processes (Aurum and Wohlin 2003; Lenz et al. 2015). Due to domain-related characteristics of requirements negotiations, they differ in terms of the role of the negotiating parties, the type of negotiation issues, and thus the decisions to be made. That is because the context of requirements negotiations depends on software project related factors. The negotiation parties in a software organisation include, on the one hand, individual people such as product manager, project manager, or architect, and, on the other hand, groups of people who represent negotiation parties such as customer, supplier, management of a company, or development team. Every stakeholder brings individual and role-specific knowledge, capabilities, and skills (Fricker and Grünbacher 2008) as well as role-dependent negotiation issues and decisions to be made during the process of requirements negotiations.

Moreover, the software project guidelines determining the software development method influence the scope and frequency of requirements negotiations. In traditional software development, requirements negotiations at the beginning of the project are essential. Requirements engineering mainly takes place at the project start defining the scope of the software project. However, the advent of agile software development (which aims at delivering software more speedily and frequently (Beck et al. 2001a)) saw software development teams deliver

---

1 Co-Author: Prof. Mareike Schoop, PhD
Reprinted by permission from Springer Nature: Springer International Publishing, Cham, Switzerland: Decision Problems in Requirements Negotiations – Identifying the Underlying Structures. In: Mareike Schoop, D. Marc Kilgour (eds.) Group Decision and Negotiation. A Socio-Technical Perspective. 17th International Conference, LNBIP 293, 2017, pp. 120-131, Annika Lenz, Mareike Schoop, available at https://link.springer.com/chapter/10.1007/978-3-319-63546-0_9

© The Editor(s) (if applicable) and The Author(s), under exclusive license to Springer Fachmedien Wiesbaden GmbH, part of Springer Nature 2020
A. Lenz, *Dynamic Decision Support for Electronic Requirements Negotiations*,
https://doi.org/10.1007/978-3-658-31175-9_3

functional software in shorter development cycles. Hence, agile software development as an iterative incremental development approach requires more frequent requirements negotiations of smaller scope based on user requirements and requirements changes (AL-Ta'ani and Razali 2013; Beck et al. 2001a).

Dedicated electronic support provides great advantages for communication and decision making in negotiations (Schoop 2010). To support decisions within these various processes of requirements negotiations, is our ultimate goal. Negotiation research provides approaches for decision support (for an overview of methods and systems see Reiser 2013). However, standard methods used to support negotiations are not straightforwardly suitable to support requirements negotiations in their present form. The decision process in requirements negotiations is a different one facing incomplete, missing and changing information throughout the process. Thus adapted solutions are required. (Lenz et al. 2015)

Requirements negotiations can be divided into the following three phases: preparation, negotiation, and settlement (Grünbacher et al. 2006; Reiser et al. 2012). In the pre-negotiation phase – whether electronically supported or not –, a vision of the decision problem needs to be developed in detail (Górecka et al. 2016). The definition of the decision problem and thus precisely structuring of the decision problem is of utmost importance, since the structure may impact the negotiation process and outcome (Mumpower 1991). In alignment with the aspect of problem-orientation of negotiation support systems, which evolved from decision support systems, the user must be helped to understand the problem structure (Kersten and Lai 2010). Moreover, only if the decision problem, which needs to be optimised (Górecka et al. 2016), is defined, electronic decision support can be provided (Simons and Tripp 2010).

To pave the way for future work on this topic, we bring the task of identifying the decision problem as one of the first, indispensable tasks in each (requirements) negotiation process into focus. Consequently, our research question is: *How is the decision problem in requirements negotiations structured?*

The overall aim is to enable decision support for one actor from an individual perspective. In this paper, the decision problem structure is investigated independently of the type of negotiation (bilateral or multilateral). In doing so, our paper firstly contributes to the preparation phase in requirements negotiations – independently if electronically supported or not – and secondly to the enablement of decision support for requirements negotiations.

To this end, we describe the structure of decision problems in the context of decision theory as well as the decision problem structure, which is supported by negotiation support systems. Subsequently, domain information which is relevant for the decision problem is identified and categorised. The resulting categories are then transferred to the decision problem context to extract the decision problem structure in requirements negotiations. A literature-based research approach has been chosen to accomplish this aim.

The remainder of this paper is structured as follows. In section 3.2, we outline the theoretical background regarding decision problems. In section 3.3, information relevant to the decision problem in requirements negotiations is described and applied to a decision problem structure following the two paradigms of software development, namely traditional requirements engineering and agile requirements engineering, resulting in a matrix to identify decision relevant information in a negotiation context. In section 3.4, our findings are briefly discussed.

3.2 Decision Problem Structure in Negotiations

A multi-criteria decision problem consists of the objective, optionally lower-level objectives, attributes, and attribute values (Keeney and Raiffa 1976). The objective of a decision problem indicates the direction to strive for. An objective can be subdivided into lower-level objectives of more detail, also called sub-objectives. The lowest-level objectives may be associated with attributes, which will indicate the degree of meeting the objective. Attributes are used to measure the objective according to their attribute values. The decision problem itself is organised in a hierarchy with infinite optional levels (Danielson and Ekenberg 2016; Keeney and Raiffa 1976).

In negotiation analysis theory, a negotiation template specifies the structure of the decision problem in detail (Górecka et al. 2016). The negotiation template design comprises of the negotiation issues and all feasible options to resolve these issues. Thus, in a negotiation context, the objective is associated with attributes, which are negotiable and to be negotiated. Such attributes are called negotiation issues. For each issue, possible resolutions are assigned, to which we refer as negotiation alternatives (Raiffa et al. 2002). We treat alternatives as negotiable values. Hence, a decision problem in negotiations is structured by an objective, negotiation issues, and negotiation alternatives, see Figure 4.

State-of-the-art negotiation support systems such as Inspire (Kersten and Noronha 1999b), Negoisst (Schoop et al. 2003; Schoop 2010), or SmartSettle (Thiessen and Soberg 2003) support such a basic decision problem structure. Such systems follow multi-attribute utility theory, predominantly utilising linear-additive utility functions, which are calculated based on an individual's preferences (Keeney and Raiffa 1976). The objective of the decision problem is to maximise the utility of a negotiation offer. A negotiation offer's utility is the sum of the partial utilities of the selected negotiation alternatives based on the

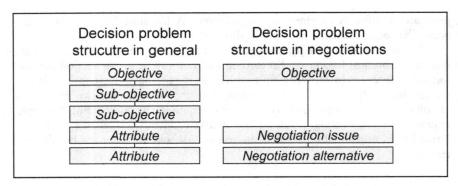

Figure 4:   Decision problem structure in general and in negotiations

corresponding negotiation issue's weight. The general decision problem structure in negotiations in conjunction with the concept of linear-additive utility functions is applied in current negotiation support systems for negotiation analysis.

3.3   Requirements Negotiations

In the following, we will investigate problem structures in requirements negotiations following two paradigms of software development methods, namely *the traditional software development method*, such as the waterfall method, abbreviated as traditional requirements negotiations (section 3.3.1), as well as the *agile software development method*, such as Scrum, abbreviated as agile requirements negotiations (section 3.3.2). In section 3.3.3 we present their implication in the form of a matrix.

3.3.1   Decision Problem Structures in Traditional Requirements Negotiations

The aim of requirements negotiations is to get an agreed-upon sound set of requirements (Lenz et al. 2015). Through requirements negotiations, stakeholders make trade-offs between the desired system functionality, the technology to be applied, the project schedule as well as project cost (Grünbacher and Seyff 2005). Thus, not only required system functions but also non-functional requirements, the technology stack, and conditions are to be negotiated (Herzwurm et al. 2012).

Packages. Packages are used for structuring reasons. Structuring may be based on functions, e.g. when requirements are bundled into features, since a software project covers a huge number of requirements.

Firstly, packages are used to assign negotiable requirements to sub-negotiations, which are conducted separately. In negotiation support systems, a hierarchy level for structuring is not yet applied. However, the objective of decision problems can be divided into sub-objectives, because of which we expand the negotiation context by a sub-objective level to cover *packages as sub-objectives*.

Secondly, packages describe negotiation issues themselves, e.g. in negotiations about whether to implement features at all or when to implement features. So, we map *packages also to negotiation issues*.

Requirements. A requirement is "(1) A condition or capability needed by a user to solve a problem or achieve an objective. (2) A condition or capability that must be met or possessed by a system or system component to satisfy a contract, standard, specification, or other formally imposed documents. (3) A documented representation of a condition or capability as in (1) or (2)." (Institute of Electrical and Electronics Engineers 1990, p. 65). This definition covers different types of requirements, namely quality requirements, and constraints (Pohl 2010). Since requirements negotiation is about negotiating requirements, *requirements are treated as negotiation issues*.

However, if the negotiation takes place on a higher level, in which packages of requirements are negotiated, the requirements themselves can be utilised to describe these packages, in which case the *requirements represent attributes*. Since these attributes are neither negotiation issues nor negotiation alternatives, but are used for description as attributes in general decision problem structures, we keep the term attribute. Since decision problems in negotiations do not yet cover such kind of attributes, the negotiation context is also expanded by attributes for negotiation issues.

Solutions. Solutions are implementation scenarios for requirements. While requirements describe the problem to be addressed in the software development process and thus specify "what" is to be developed, solutions describe the solution space to this problem, and thus specify "how" it is to be developed. (Pohl 2010)

Therefore, considering requirements as negotiation issues, *solutions describe negotiation alternatives* (Herzwurm et al. 2012). Solutions may cover a single requirement or a whole package. The latter is the case, for example when choosing technologies to be deployed, which hold for a whole package (Franch and Carvallo 2002). Hence, if packages are formulated as negotiation issues, *solutions address negotiation alternatives* as well.

Criteria. In requirements negotiations, requirements are assessed in preparation for decision making. This has the benefit that the decision makers can assign their preferences based on the assessment rather than assigning their preferences directly to the requirements. In some approaches providing decision support, requirements are assessed with respect to their business value and development effort (Boehm et al. 2001; Ruhe et al. 2002). Other approaches leave the criteria definition to the project stakeholders. In this case, they generate relevant criteria at the beginning of the negotiation, e.g. by an initial brainstorming (In and Olson 2004). The above-mentioned two-level approach, prioritises features with respect to business goals of the organisation and utilises ease of realisation and business value to prioritise low-level requirements (Kukreja and Boehm 2013). Thakurta (2017) identifies a plethora of thirteen requirements attributes, which influence requirements prioritisation. Thus, *criteria address requirements as attributes for negotiation issues.*

However, criteria may also be used to assess packages directly. Likewise, criteria for packages facilitate the decision maker to decide on a better valuation basis. Compared with criteria for requirements, criteria for packages have the advantage that information does not need to be elicited in such detail. So, *criteria for packages also represent attributes for negotiation issues.*

Criteria may also be applied to solutions for assessment reasons. Thus, criteria may also be used to *describe solutions* and hence used as *attributes to describe negotiation alternatives.*

Criteria are also used to define overall project constraints or contract conditions, such as project duration or project budget. In this case, criteria are negotiable themselves and thus, formulated as *negotiation issues* among requirements and solutions (Herzwurm et al. 2012).

Possible Decision Problem Structures. From above, different decision problem structures following traditional software development methods can be derived, see Figure 5. We observe semantic differences in the negotiation context but also differences in the hierarchical structure of different scenarios. Negotiation

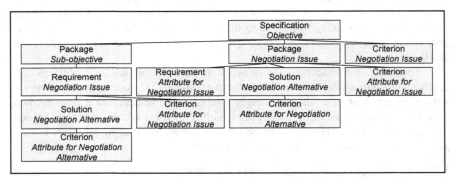

Figure 5:   Possible decision problem structures in traditional requirements negotiations

support systems allow only a two-level structure of negotiation issues and alternatives (e.g. Schoop et al. 2003; Schoop 2010). However, the number of levels in requirements negotiations is potentially higher than in usual negotiations due to domain characteristics. Thus, current negotiation support systems do not completely facilitate decision support for requirements negotiations.

3.3.2   Decision Problem Structures in Agile Requirements Negotiations

Agile software development claims to deliver working software early and more frequently as well as collaborate closely with the customer to satisfy the customer (Beck et al. 2001b). Fulfilling these aims, the requirements engineering process needs to be adapted to accomplish its goals (Ramesh et al. 2010). The difference of the requirements engineering process in traditional software methods and in agile software methods, however, is not that it would include different activities, but that in agile requirements engineering the requirements engineering activities take place iteratively in each development cycle, namely requirements elicitation, documentation, and validation as well as negotiation, and are not sequential but intermingled and addressed together. (Ramesh et al. 2010)

Nonetheless, in the pre-negotiation phase, the decision problem, which is to be negotiated, must be identified. This is done in a more extensive manner for the first negotiation, while in each iteration, the decision problem may be derived from already identified negotiation issues (from the product backlog or the sprint backlog) or from changed negotiation issues.

In the requirements analysis and negotiation activities, the focus is on refining, changing, and prioritising requirements (Ramesh et al. 2010). These activities are performed during assembling the backlog, which contains a list of items, which are desired to be implemented (Clarke and Kautz 2014). The backlog items cover requirements, which are in general specified in user stories (Clarke and Kautz 2014; Inayat et al. 2015). These requirements are argued to be negotiable (Clarke and Kautz 2014). From the product backlog, the release backlog is derived, which covers a fragment of the required functionality (Clarke and Kautz 2014). Based on the release backlog, the sprint backlog defines the requirements, which are to be implemented in the next sprint (Clarke and Kautz 2014). Hence, release planning, and sprint planning, in which the requirements bundles are negotiated, which are implemented in the next release, respectively in the next sprint are main activities.

Some studies claim that the product owner is responsible for prioritisation of the backlog (e.g. Moe et al. 2012), however others argue that (in the sprint planning), product managers and developers negotiate backlog items (Vlaanderen et al. 2011). Especially, if different customer groups are involved, who are

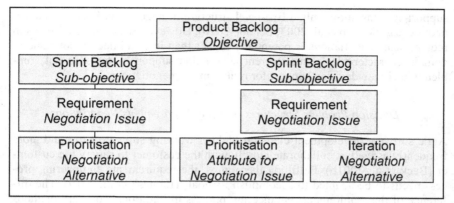

Figure 6:   Possible decision problem structures in agile requirements negotiations

concerned about different required functionality, negotiation is performed (Ramesh et al. 2010). Hence, main negotiation activities in each development cycle comprise to seek consensus about the *prioritisation of requirements* according to their business value or risk (Inayat et al. 2015) and accordingly their *assignment* to iterations.

In contrast to traditional requirements negotiations, these negotiations concern rather the "what" dimension (what is to be implemented) than the how dimension (Inayat et al. 2015). Thus, in the case of prioritisation, the backlog covers the objective *(product backlog – objective*; *sprint backlog – sub-objective)*, the *requirements the negotiation issues*, and *their prioritisation*, which is negotiated among the involved stakeholders, covers the *negotiation alternatives*.

In the assignment negotiation, the respective backlog covers as well the *sub-objective*, and the *requirements the negotiation issues*. Here, the *prioritisation applies* as criteria for the requirements and thus, *attributes for negotiation issues*, while the *iteration covers the negotiation alternatives* in terms of to which iteration the requirements are assigned (or if it is assigned to the next iteration, or if at all). Figure 6 shows possible decision problem structures in agile requirements negotiations.

Applied to the terminology identified in section 3.3.1, the product backlog represents the specification, the release, and sprint backlog represent a package, the prioritisation represents a criterion, and the iteration represents a solution.

3.3.3   Matrix of Possible Decision Problem Structures

In section 3.2, we found out that a decision problem in general may consist of the objective, sub-objectives, and attributes, whereas the decision problem in negotiations consists of an objective, negotiation issues, and negotiation alternatives. From the above described decision-relevant information in the domain context, which is categorised into packages, requirements, solutions, and criteria, we develop the following matrix to transfer these categories into a negotiation context, see Table 1.

This matrix allows to determine relevant decision problem structures in requirements negotiations and shows that in certain scenarios, the negotiation context needs to be expanded by a structuring level and/or by a level, which provides more information.

Regarding this diversity, there is no unique approach to apply a decision problem structure to the decision problem to be solved. From a customer's perspective, one could base the decision on a set of requirements on cost and time. Other decision makers may prefer to base their decision on how the requirements are implemented (i.e. the architectural design) rather than cost and time. A developer's perspective might rather include available resources. Consequently, there is more than one way to design and structure the decision problem.

Table 1:   Matrix of possible decision problem structures in requirements negotiations. GDP: General decision problem structure in negotiations; TRN: In traditional requirements negotiations; ARN: In agile requirements negotiations.

	GDP		GDP	GDP		
	Objective	Sub-objective	Negotiation Issue	Negotiation Alternative	Attribute for Negotiation Issue	Attribute for Negotiation Alternative
Specification	TRN, ARN					
Package		TRN, ARN	TRN			
Requirement			TRN, ARN			
Criterion			TRN	ARN	TRN, ARN	TRN

3.4   Discussion and Conclusion

We have shown that there is no uniform overall decision problem structure for requirements negotiations. The developed possible decision problem structures in requirements negotiations and their resulting matrix facilitates to accomplish the identification of the decision problem of the use case at hand during the pre-negotiation phase. This task is of prime importance, independently if requirements negotiations are carried out with electronic support or without (Simons and Tripp 2010). In requirements negotiation, where teams are dispersed, electronic support of the pre-negotiation phase is of great benefit. Where this task is performed face to face, which is often the case in agile requirements negotiation (Inayat et al. 2015; Ramesh et al. 2010), the advantages of electronic media can be exploited using synchronous tools (e.g. like the EasyWinWin approach; Boehm and Kitapci 2006). Moreover, synergies can be enabled by providing interfaces to requirements management and software development tools to complement requirements negotiation support systems. Furthermore, it is suggested not to support requirements negotiations electronically using a single medium, but support them by a mix of media (Damian et al. 2008).

   We chose a literature-based approach. Thus, one limitation of our approach is that our results reflect only those requirements negotiations concepts and approaches that have been published. However, the literature utilised builds inter alia upon empirical results. Therefore, this limitation is negligible.

   Current requirements negotiation systems providing decision support can be grouped into automated approaches, recommender systems, and interactive approaches (for an overview see Lenz et al. 2016). Automated approaches negotiate autonomously based on criteria specified prior to the negotiation process. Recommender systems provide recommendations for group decision making during requirements negotiations, e.g. (Felfernig et al. 2012). Interactive decision support in requirements negotiations utilises an analytic hierarchy process (e.g. Ruhe et al. 2002) or simple additive weighting approaches (e.g. variants of the EasyWinWin approach; In and Olson 2004). In this group, some systems (such as Boehm et al. 2001; Ruhe et al. 2002) require the fixed criteria business value and ease of realisation, whilst other (such as In and Olson 2004) provide the opportunity to define individual criteria. Thus, the support level of these three groups is a different one. However, what all approaches have in common is that they assume a certain structure of the decision problem. EasyWinWin approaches apply requirements (i.e. win conditions), solutions (i.e. resolution options), and criteria. A two-level approach, based on EasyWinWin and utilising TOPSIS, includes packages (Kukreja and Boehm 2013). Each system supports one and only one decision problem structure, which is presumed for each negotiation.

Negotiation of criteria in terms of contract conditions such as the price is not considered in these approaches. They focus on the negotiation of requirements.

Requirements negotiation systems which do not presume a specific decision problem structure focus on supporting group collaboration or enhancing participation (e.g. Kukreja 2012; Renzel et al. 2013; van de Walle et al. 2007).

The variability of the decision problem structure makes it difficult to provide decision support in requirements negotiations. The more flexible the decision support approach, i.e. the more scenarios it can support, the more complex both development and usage of such a system are. From this point of view, it is to consider, which scenarios to concentrate on, e.g. based on their importance or frequency. To develop a system, which supports reasonable decision problems in traditional and agile requirements negotiations, is our ultimate goal and the present paper contributes to its conceptual design.

3.5 Acknowledgements

The authors wish to acknowledge the valuable comments and suggestions made by the anonymous reviewers and gratefully acknowledge the funding provided by the Faculty of Business, Economics, and Social Sciences at the University of Hohenheim within the research area "Negotiation Research – Transformation, Technology, Media, and Costs".

4 Assessment of Multi-Criteria Preference Measurement Methods for a Dynamic Environment[2]

4.1 Introduction

Decision making with multiple objectives is required in a wide range of domains. To support such multi-criteria decision making, a plethora of methods for measuring the decision maker's preferences have been developed. The aim of preference measurement methods is to assess feasible alternatives for the decision maker to support his/her decision making. Usually, preference measurement methods assume a static context (Benítez et al. 2012). Such approaches require the decision maker to provide all preference information at the time of measurement. In other words, a one-shot preference measurement is performed without considering changes.

However, in many cases, the decision maker does not have complete knowledge at the time when preference measurement is necessary. Dynamic decision making problems with multiple, conflicting objectives appear in many real-world scenarios (Helbig et al. 2016), e.g. optimising traffic (Nebro et al. 2018), replacements configurations for multi-component systems (Certa et al. 2013), surgical patients' prioritisation (Abbasgholizadeh Rahimi et al. 2016), or decision support in negotiations (Kersten et al. 1990). In the following, we explain preference changes in a dynamic context using the example of negotiations. In negotiations a variety of decisions must be made. To have an adequate basis for decision making, i.e. articulate, assess, and com-pare offers, preferences must be measured very early, in fact prior to the actual negotiation phase.

Negotiation processes are shaped and influenced by their dynamic nature. They are interdependent processes between different parties, which implies that a negotiator is influenced by and must rely on his/her partner. Thus, they are in a two-way process that does not give them sole control. This reciprocity means

2 Co-Author: Prof. Mareike Schoop, PhD
  The content of this chapter is already published as: Annika Lenz, Mareike Schoop, 2019, Assessment of Multi-Criteria Preference Measurement Methods for a Dynamic Environment. In: Tung Bui (ed.) Proceedings of the 52nd Hawaii International Conference on System Sciences, pp 1803–1812, available at http://hdl.handle.net/10125/59620

A. Lenz, *Dynamic Decision Support for Electronic Requirements Negotiations*, https://doi.org/10.1007/978-3-658-31175-9_4

that the parties must exchange views and information in order to reach a joint solution. The exchange process takes place iteratively and builds on the previous exchange. This way both partners gain new information during the process.

This new information in turn influences the shape of the negotiation itself. For example, parties might find out or wish for themselves that they should negotiate more issues than they had previously assumed. This means, the scope of the negotiation and therewith the decision problem is changed. By the change of the scope, i.e. introducing new attributes, new alternatives, or withdrawing attributes or alternatives, preferences articulated at the beginning of a negotiation are obsolete. Furthermore, whilst maintaining the same agenda throughout the negotiation, preferences might change simply by being provided with new information, having more clarity in the process, or by process dynamics (Curhan et al. 2004; Vetschera 2007) according to dissonance theory (Festinger 1957) and reactance theory (Brehm and Brehm 1981). Dissonance theory proposes that negotiators perceive the value of their outcome, i.e. the offer chosen, higher in retrospective (Curhan et al. 2004; Vetschera 2007), while reactance theory postulates that alternatives are perceived more attractive if they are jeopardised to be forfeited and vice versa (Curhan et al. 2004; Vetschera 2007). This means that even if information is not outdated, negotiators may desire to readjust their preferences due to the negotiation process dynamics. In general, preference formation, learning or fatigue may cause preference dynamics (Netzer et al. 2008).

To sum up, by change of scope, increase of information level, or process dynamics, preferences change. As outlined in the example, the need for dynamic, interactive methods becomes clear (Helbig et al. 2016; Nebro et al. 2018). However, such dynamic, interactive approaches are still scarce, since these methods must take a new dimension into account: time (Benítez et al. 2012; Nebro et al. 2018). The considered decision problems are time-dependent as soon as new knowledge affects the decisional context: attributes, alternatives, or preference information. In many practical situations it is unachievable to provide preference information for all decision elements involved beforehand (Benítez et al. 2012). New methods try to take incomplete or imprecise preference information into account (e.g. Guo et al. 2003; Reiser 2013; Roszkowska and Wachowicz 2015a). However, literature on interactive, dynamic methods is still scarce (Nebro et al. 2018).

Our aim is to investigate to what extent interactive, multi-criteria preference measurement approaches are suitable in a dynamic environment. We analyse the methods' potential to be extended to allow for dynamic preference adjustment. Helping a decision maker to fine-tune his/her preferences in an environment where the decision context itself changes over time, is challenging, especially when a high number of objectives is involved (Nebro et al. 2018). We, therefore, follow a three-step approach to reach this aim:

Research question 1: What are the requirements for individual interactive dynamic preference measurement?

Research question 2: Do preference measurement methods address the requirements identified?

Research question 3: What potential do preference measurement methods have to be expanded to fit dynamic demands?

We hereby focus on preference measurement for an individual decision maker. The method must allow interactivity (cf. Nebro et al. 2018), to allow the decision maker to redefine his/her preferences according to an increasing knowledge.

To answer our research questions, we derive general requirements for such a method and select methods, which are supposed to meet the identified requirements. To assess the selected methods, we follow a mixed-methods approach, which both qualitatively evaluates the fulfilment of the identified requirements as well as their expandability to handle preference adjustments and quantitatively evaluates their performance regarding common preference measurement criteria, i.e. validity, efficiency, and complexity. Both the qualitative and quantitative assessment are utilised to select the best suitable method to be extended by dynamic means.

To this end, this paper is structured as follows. In section 4.2, we outline theoretical background on preference measurement methods and related work on dynamic preference measurement. Section 4.3 identifies relevant requirements for dynamic preference measurement and selects promising methods. The selected methods are assessed by their fulfilment of the identified requirements and evaluated in section 4.4. Section 4.5 concludes this paper and gives a brief outlook.

4.2 Theoretical Background and Related Work

A multitude of approaches exists to assess alternatives respectively choose the 'best' alternative. In this chapter, we review general approaches based on multi-attribute utility theory (Keeney and Raiffa 1976) and preference measurement methods, which take a temporal perspective.

4.2.1 Utility Based Multi-Criteria Decision Analysis Approaches

Multi-criteria decision analysis methods comprise of a plethora of approaches. Apart from outranking methods (e.g. the ELECTRE family (Roy 1990) or PROMETHEE family (Brans and Vincke 1985)), fuzzy methods, multi-objective optimisation, robust ordinal regression methods (Greco et al. 2008), and UTA methods (Jacquet-Lagreze and Siskos 1982), we focus on approaches, which provide the possibility to assess all alternatives in a multi-criteria decision problem in terms of utility applying multi-attribute utility theory (Keeney and Raiffa 1976).

In concordance with multi-attribute utility theory, different utility functions can be applied (French et al. 2009). We concentrate on a linear-additive utility function by which the utility of a chosen set of alternatives is calculated by the sum of utility values u for an alternative x_i of the attribute i weighted by the relative importance w_i of the attribute i.

$$U(A) = \sum_i w_i * u(x_i) \tag{1}$$

A rough categorisation of utility based methods, which allow assessment of all alternatives mainly driven by marketing research is the division into decompositional (conjoint analyses (Green and Srinivasan 1990; Gustafsson et al. 2007)), compositional (self-explicated approaches, AHP (Lai 1995; Saaty 1990)), and hybrid approaches (Green 1984).

Conjoint analysis estimates the customer's preferences, "given his or her overall evaluations of a set of alternatives that are prespecified in terms of levels of different attributes" (Green and Srinivasan 1990, p. 4). While a disadvantage of conjoint analysis has been that it results in an information overload for the respondent using a large number of attributes (Green and Srinivasan 1990), newer methods and its applications have overcome this shortcoming (cf. Netzer et al. 2008).

The self-explicated approach is a compositional approach (Green and Srinivasan 1990), which questions the respondent separately on each attribute (stage 1) and on the attribute importance weights (stage 2). Thereby, it minimises the information-overload problem (Srinivasan and Park 1997). Hence, the traditional self-explicated approach can handle a large number of attributes and levels (Netzer et al. 2008).

Hybrid approaches have been developed aiming to combine the benefits of conjoint measurement and self-explicated methods (Green and Srinivasan 1990; Srinivasan and Park 1997). They comprise of both a self-explicated stage and a decompositional stage taking results of the previous stage into account and/or calibrating resulting preferences from both stages (Sawtooth Software, Inc. 2007).

4.2.2   Dynamic Multi-Criteria Decision Analysis Methods

Current research streams for time-dependent preference measurement comprise of methods, which allow preference adjustment without changing objectives and alternatives of the decision problem, evolutionary dynamic multi-objective optimisation using big data, dynamic adjustment of feasible alternatives, and periodic interactive verification.

Reiser (2013) develops an approach, which considers incomplete and uncertain information at the time of preference measurement. He suggests a two-part approach. As long as information is incomplete he uses Fast Polyhedral Adaptive Conjoint Estimation (FastPACE, Toubia et al. 2003) to gradually complete preference information. At the point the information level has increased to a sufficient degree, he applies ex post preference measurement using Adaptive Self-Explication (ASE, Netzer and Srinivasan 2011). Reiser (2013) focuses on incomplete and uncertain information of importance weightings and preferences for alternatives. The scope of the decision problem remains the same throughout the process.

In evolutionary dynamic multi-objective optimisation, the goal is to "find the set of trade-off solutions that is as close as possible to the set of optimal trade-off solutions" (Helbig et al. 2016, p. 1256). Nebro et al. (2018) develop an interactive approach in dynamic context for multi-objective optimisation. They use evolutionary algorithms based on reference points, which can be modified interactively, to handle changes in the environment. The overall goal is to solve an optimisation problem by the best suitable solution.

Certa et al. (2013) aim to dynamically support a decision maker in the domain of replacement configurations for multi-component systems. Dynamic updates capture changes of information about the decisional context. Their goal, too, is to find an optimal solution. They use a two-step approach comprising of obtaining the set of non-dominated trade-off solutions and comparing them to select the best one. These steps are repeated sequentially to include information about the decision problem. ELECTRE III (Roy 1990) is used to select the best solution at the time required.

Abbasgholizadeh Rahimi et al. (2016) develop a dynamic framework, considering risks and uncertainties in the context of surgical patients' prioritisation. The dynamic aspect is that patients are added and removed from waiting lists as well as their condition evolves over time, which needs to be evaluated. Their three-step framework covers defining the decision problem structure and attributes, defining and evaluating alternatives and finally a dynamic evaluation of the alternatives on a periodic update basis, while the objectives and importance weightings remain the same.

Benítez et al. (2012) use AHP (Saaty 1990) extended by the time dimension. Calculation of importance weighting is based on pairwise comparisons.

Their focus is on ensuring the consistency of information gathered by the pairwise comparisons. Preference information is allowed to be provided at several times.

Roszkowska and Wachowicz (2015a) consider preference measurement respectively decision support for ill-defined decision problems in negotiations. They apply fuzzy TOPSIS to an ill-structured negotiation problem. Their aim is to maintain a stable preference model, which is based on the aspiration level and reservation level only, throughout the negotiation process. They do not consider preference changes, but focus on taking new offers into account, which lie outside of the initially defined negotiation space. They suggest solutions to evaluate such out-of-space offers without affecting the evaluation of prior exchanged offers. In such a case, the fuzzy TOPSIS algorithm is applied without involvement of the decision maker.

In contrast, DeSarbo et al. (2005) and Liechty et al. (2005) focus on preference changes respectively preference adjustment due to several factors such as learning, exposure to additional information, fatigue, and cognitive limitations. They develop a Bayesian dynamic linear methodology to capture dynamic adjustment processes, which allows for heterogeneous level estimation.

Guo et al. (2003) consider agents to learn the negotiator's preferences to be applied in multi-attribute negotiations. They develop an algorithm, which enables agents to learn their users' preference structures over time and build a multi-attribute utility function.

To this end, dynamic preference measurement methods which cover big data approaches (e.g. Nebro et al. 2018), evolutionary algorithms (e.g. Guo et al. 2003; Nebro et al. 2018), methods, which solve optimisation problems (e.g. Certa et al. 2013; Nebro et al. 2018), or use outranking approaches (e.g. Certa et al. 2013), have been proposed.

Since it is very difficult and complex to measure preferences dynamically (Nebro et al. 2018), new methods for this purpose focus on certain aspects of the dynamic decisional context. Of the interactive ones for an individual decision maker, which provide the possibility of assessing all alternatives in terms of utility, dynamic methods focus either on changes of the decision scope (e.g. Roszkowska and Wachowicz 2015a) without preference changes, alternative and alternative assessment changes (e.g. Abbasgholizadeh Rahimi et al. 2016), preference development (e.g. Reiser 2013), or focus on consistency issues of additional paired comparisons (e.g. Benítez et al. 2012).

4.3   Selection of an Adequate Preference Measurement Method

In this chapter, we identify requirements for an individual, interactive dynamic preference measurement method and develop an evaluation scale. Moreover, we select six methods, which will be analysed towards their suitability in a dynamic environment.

4.3.1   Requirements and Assessment Scale

We derive the following requirements for a preference measurement method to capture a dynamic environment. The benefit of dynamic preference measurement is to enable dynamic decision support, which is usually provided for an individual decision maker (cf. Raiffa et al. 2002). As the analysis of a set of attributes is an individual's task, or the task of a homogeneous group of stakeholders (e.g. Felfernig et al. 2012), individual preference measurement is required. Thus, the method must be able to estimate preferences for an individual decision maker (Req1).

The focus of this paper is to evaluate preference measurement methods by their suitability for dynamic preference measurement. Therefore, the preference measurement method must be able to handle changes in the scope of the decision problem (Req2), i.e. changes of attributes and alternatives (cf. Fernandes 2016). It must handle modification of attributes and alternatives, namely efficient adding and withdrawing must be possible.

Along with the change of scope, preferences for additional elements must be complemented without distorting existing preferences and if possible, without the necessity to measure all preferences again. Equally, deleting objectives or attributes must not affect valid preferences for the remaining objectives and attributes (Req3).

Moreover, if the scope of the decision problem remains the same throughout the process, preferences regarding the objectives or attributes may change nonetheless (cf. Vetschera 2007). Hence, the preference measurement method must be able to adjust the initially elicited preferences efficiently (Req4).

The methods are assessed, if they fulfil ('+') or do not fulfil ('-') the requirements Req1 - Req4. If the methods do not meet the specified requirements sufficiently, we will evaluate them on a scale from '--' to '++', how well they can be expanded to meet the requirements, i.e. allow efficient individual dynamic preference adjustment. A negative assessment means that the method cannot be expanded to adjust preferences dynamically, neutral assessment means that an expansion for dynamic preference adjustment is possible, but the preference adjustment requires high effort, while positive assessment means that the method can be expanded for efficient dynamic preference adjustment. We differentiate between two levels in both the negative and the positive range to indicate the effort required for dynamic preference adjustment.

4.3.2 Selection of Methods

To meet the requirements, we elicit state-of-the-art preference measurement methods, which allow individual preference measurement. Self-explicated approaches are well suited to measure preferences for multi-attribute products that involve a large number of attributes (Netzer and Srinivasan 2011; Schlereth et al. 2014). In recent years, new self-explicated methods have been suggested, which include an adaptive question design to reduce effort for the decision maker (Reiser 2013).

ASE by Netzer and Srinivasan (2011) is a newer compositional preference measurement approach with adaptive question design. It is designed to solve the self-explicated constant sum question problem when the number of product attributes becomes large (Netzer and Srinivasan 2011). The preferences for alternatives are elicited by rating them on a defined rating scale. The relative attribute importance weightings are elicited by first ranking the attributes according to their importance and second comparing pairs of attributes. The pairwise comparisons are chosen adaptively based on their potential to provide the most information.

An extension of ASE is the Presorted Adaptive Self-Explicated Approach (PASE) by Schlereth et al. (2014). It is also a self-explicated approach of adaptive character. Additionally to ASE, it proposes to rate the attributes according to their importance prior to the attribute ranking in order to presort them. They argue that positioning a task, which is not trade-off based, simplifies the subsequent trade-off based task. A presorted list of attributes is supposed to reduce the cognitive burden in the ranking task.

The Paired Comparison-based Preference Measurement (PCPM) by Scholz et al. (2010) is an alternative compositional approach using constant-sum paired comparison questions. PCPM (Scholz et al. 2010) utilises AHP to estimate part worths, but reduces the set of pairwise comparisons. The overall decision problem is divided into subproblems on different levels, for which preferences are elicited. The question design aims to compare each attribute (alternative) with four other attributes (alternatives) to reduce the number of comparisons. Missing preference relations are calculated based on known comparison information.

It is argued that new self-explicated approaches are superior over conjoint analyses regarding a high number of attributes, usability for respondents or ease in terms of data collection (e.g. Matzner et al. 2015). However, to gain comprehensive insights, we include the Conjoint Adaptive Ranking Database (CARDS) by Dahan (2007) as a newer conjoint analysis, which follows an adaptive design. The main concept of CARDS builds on two ideas (Dahan et al. 2004): to measure the decision maker's elimination process by identifying his/her simplification decision rule and thus consider only key attributes; and to avoid inconsistent answers by guiding the decision maker towards consistent answers. During the process, inconsistent product combinations are eliminated as soon as they are classified as the same.

Hybrid methods are designed to combine the best of self-explicated and conjoint approaches. The Adaptive Conjoint Analysis (ACA) is an adaptive method developed by Johnson (1987) and enhanced by Sawtooth Software, Inc. (2007). It follows a hybrid approach and enjoys large popularity among researchers and practitioners (Meißner et al. 2011). In the compositional stage, both the desirability of alternatives (Sawtooth Software, Inc. 2007) and the relative attribute importance across attributes are rated. Self-explicated part worths are calculated (Netzer and Srinivasan 2011). The decompositional stage builds on results of the compositional stage. Paired-comparison trade-off questions are asked to compare up to five attributes updating the utility estimates (Sawtooth Software, Inc. 2007). The paired-comparison questions are adaptively chosen based on estimated utility, the question design, and the frequency of attributes compared. The resulting estimates of both stages are combined based on a weighting factor.

FastPACE by Toubia et al. (2003) is a state-of-the-art hybrid method with adaptive comparison tasks at an individual level. It is built on ACA with the aim of an efficient design of the adaption of new stimuli. The aim is to reduce the number of product combinations by polyhedral question design. It combines the self-explicated approach with conjoint analysis by graded paired comparisons of partial product profiles, which are chosen adaptively (Netzer and Srinivasan 2011).

To this end, the methods we will evaluate in this paper cover three self-explicated approaches (ASE, PASE, PCPM), one conjoint analysis (CARDS), and two hybrid approaches (Fast-PACE, ACA).

4.4 Assessment of Selected Methods

In this chapter, we will assess the selected methods using a mixed-methods approach. In section 4.4.1, we will qualitatively analyse, if these methods address the requirements, respectively how well they can be expanded to fulfil them. The methods are quantitatively analysed towards their performance, i.e. efficiency, validity, and difficulty, in section 4.4.2.

4.4.1   Qualitative Fulfilment of Requirements

In the following, we analyse the selected methods towards their fulfilment of the identified requirements. ASE, PASE, PCPM, CARDS, FastPACE and ACA all are applicable for an individual decision maker (Req1). None of the methods requires preferences of other respondents with similar preference profiles.

The requirement to handle changes in the scope of the decision problem (Req2) is not addressed by the methods. None of them stipulates to add or withdraw objectives or attributes.

Since none of the methods stipulates attribute or value changes, preference elicitation of new attributes and values respectively preference adjustment of remaining attributes and values (Req3) is not considered.

Regarding preference adjustment due to preference changes independently of attribute and alternative changes (e.g. due to an increasing information level, Req4), CARDS does not stipulate preference changes. Beyond that, it does not use inconsistent answers to review elicited preferences, but to reduce the response error by deleting inconsistent response options (Dahan et al. 2004). In PCPM, adjustments of preferences are stipulated neither. PCPM utilises a fixed question design for comparisons, which does neither suggest how to determine comparisons in case of new/obsolete attributes/alternatives nor does it provide possibilities for additional comparisons in case of preference changes. In ACA and FastPACE, update mechanisms for part worths exist. This is done by conducting new set(s) of comparisons. After each set of comparisons, the part worths are updated. However, a deletion of obsolete preferences is not stipulated, so the initial preferences would be considered as well. Regarding ASE and PASE new comparisons can be conducted, if preference changes occur. The estimation of the part worths is done after each set of comparisons taking all information into account. So in case of changes, the calculation can be applied as it is provided in ASE already. However likewise as in ACA and FastPACE and as in all one-shot methods, deletion of outdated information is not stipulated.

Regarding the possibility to expand the methods to fit dynamic demands, CARDS focuses on key attributes, which is contradictory to the aim of an expansion, because it is supposed to assess all attributes. The main concept of CARDS is to eliminate less important attributes and inconsistent response options. Thus, if changes force the addition or deletion of attributes or alternatives, the method must be conducted from scratch. In PCPM, expansion is possible in principle. However because of the fixed question design, changes require very high effort. Even deletion of attributes/alternatives requires to conduct new comparisons and entails a number of recalculations. In ACA, scaling in stage 1 must be repeated based on the original scores. In stage 2, additional comparisons must be determined and asked. The mechanism to update preference information is of limited usage, since in case of deletion, outdated information must be deleted and thus the calculation of utility estimated redone from scratch. Moreover, because of rescaling in stage 1, the combination of estimates of stage 1 and stage 2 must be recalculated. Since FastPACE builds on ACA, but focuses on the improvement of the question design, the expansion is similar to ACA.

Expansion of ASE and PASE is possible. The single steps rating of alternative desirabilities, rating of attributes (in case of PASE), and ranking of attributes can be repeated for new at-tributes and/or alternatives. Subsequently, new attributes and alternatives (in case of new best or worst alternatives) require new attribute comparisons. In case of attribute or alternative deletion, the respective comparison information can be deleted from the elicited preferences. Deletion may also result in new attribute comparisons. If attributes and values remain the same, but their preferences change, the elicited preference information may be deleted, and consequently the elicitation steps for single attributes or alternatives repeated as well as new attribute comparisons conducted. In each case, the part worths may be estimated after the respective set of attribute comparisons utilising all secured preference information.

Table 2 gives an overview of the assessment of the methods to evaluate. The methods differ in the possibility of an efficient expansion. Since CARDS does not show potential to be expand-ed, it will be excluded from further consideration. Both ASE and PASE show the most potential for expansion.

Table 2: Assessment of requirements. *) New information can be considered during the elicitation.

Method	Fulfilment of requirements				Possibility to expand
	Req1	Req2	Req3	Req4	
ASE	+	-	-	+*)	++
PASE	+	-	-	+*)	++
PCPM	+	-	-	-	o
ACA	+	-	-	+*)	+
FastPACE	+	-	-	+*)	+
CARDS	+	-	-	-	--

4.4.2   Quantitative Performance Assessment

In the following, the selected methods are evaluated based on validity (convergent validity, discriminant validity, and predictive validity), efficiency, and complexity to ensure that the best suitable methods do not suffer major shortcomings regarding state-of-the-art performance criteria.

CARDS was shown to be not suitable for efficient expansion by dynamic means. Hence, in the following only ACA, FastPACE, ASE, PASE, and PCPM are assessed. For this purpose, we discuss recent studies by Schlereth et al. (2014), who evaluate ASE, PASE, and PCPM; Meißner et al. (2011), who evaluate ACA, ASE, and PCPM; and Netzer and Srinivasan (2011), who evaluate ACA, FastPACE, and ASE.

We assess the methods in relation to each other according to the empirical evaluation in the original studies. Thus, we use a relative scale from '--' to '++', negative/positive range meaning worse/better than other method(s) evaluated in the respective measures.

4.4.2.1 Validity

Regarding convergent validity, Schlereth et al. (2014) report high correlations for the attribute importance weights across ASE and PASE (>0.75, PCPM n.a.) in their first survey and also high correlations for ASE, PCPM, and PASE (>0.65) in their second survey (Schlereth et al. 2014). In line with these results, Meißner et al. (2011) report high correlations of ACA and ASE (0.84), ACA and PCPM (0.84), and ASE and PCPM (0.89). Thus, high convergent validity is assumed for all evaluated methods.

Discriminant validity is measured between attribute importance weights by the range between most and least important attributes at a measurement method level. ASE, PASE, and PCPM show the best discriminant validity among all of the evaluated methods (Schlereth et al. 2014). Discriminant validity across respondents (measured by average dispersion across respondents) is reported for ASE (M SD in first survey = 9.07, M SD in second survey = 9.66) and PASE (M SD in first survey = 9.43, M SD in second survey = 9.50) as very high, and PCPM still high (first survey n.a., M SD in second survey = 5.96) (Schlereth et al. 2014). Discriminant validity across individuals for ASE and PCPM is reported as much higher than for ACA (Meißner et al. 2011), measured by the dispersion of the attribute importance weights. Moreover, the variance of the attribute importance weights is significantly different for only one case between ASE and PCPM, while it is different between ACA and PCPM for 12 cases and between ACA and ASE for 11 cases, which means that the divergent importance of attributes is captured better by ASE and PCPM (Meißner et al. 2011).

Predictive validity is measured differently in the empirical studies applied. Schlereth et al. (2014) measure predictive validity (1) by hit rates of predicting the first-choice of three alter-natives in four holdout tasks; (2) perceived quality of importance weights, for which respondents rated how well the importance weights determined matched their true importance weights; (3) hit rate for the identification of own importance weights among the set of four alternative importance weights. (1) shows low significant superiority of PASE compared to

ASE in their first survey, however, no significant difference of PASE, ASE, and PCPM in their second survey. (2) shows significant difference of PASE compared to ASE in their first survey, however no significant difference of ASE, PASE, and PCPM in their second survey. (3) shows low significant difference of PASE compared to ASE, and high significant difference of PCPM to ASE, while there is no significant difference of PCPM and PASE. Netzer and Srinivasan (2011) measure individual-level predictive validity by (1) the hit rates of predicting the highest-ranked alternative in each of the two validation sets (choice set hit rate); (2) the hit rate for the 12 pairwise choices derived from the ranking of four alternatives in their two choice sets; (3) average rank-order correlation between predicted and actual ranking for each respondent. Each three measures show that ACA and FastPACE have significantly lower predictive validity than ASE. Meißner et al. (2011) report no significant differences between their evaluated methods for the hit rate of the best alternative, however, report a low significant difference of PCPM compared to ACA for the hit rate of the ranking of alternatives.

4.4.2.2 Efficiency

Mixed results are reported regarding the effort a respondent expends on the preference measurement tasks. ASE is significantly shorter than PASE in the first survey of Schlereth et al. (2014) except for the ranking task, however, no significant differences are reported for their second survey. The survey duration using PCPM is significantly shorter than using ASE and PASE (Schlereth et al. 2014). Meißner et al. (2011) report an average duration of 6.51 mins for PCPM, 8.10 mins for ASE, and 12.78 mins for ACA, while Netzer and Srinivasan (2011) report ACA as fastest (14.45 mins), followed by ASE (15.10 mins) and FastPACE (21.60 mins). They assume a delay of six to eight seconds between the paired comparison questions resulting from using interpreted code to be responsible for the significant longer duration of FastPACE.

However, Schlereth et al. (2014) argue that if methods stay below the mark of 20 mins, the effort associated is unlikely overwhelming for respondents. Therefore, all evaluated methods except for FastPACE, probably due to implementation issues, are well suited.

4.4.2.3 Survey difficulty

Survey complexity of ASE and PASE is considered equally high, but differs significantly to PCPM, which is perceived easier than ASE and PASE (Schlereth et al. 2014). Contrary, Meißner et al. (2011) report for task difficulty that ASE is significantly better than ACA and PCPM. Regarding ASE, ACA, and FastPACE no significant differences in difficulty are reported.

However, all methods – where ratings are reported – are perceived as rather of low complexity, because ASE, PASE, and PCPM are evaluated on an average > 4 at a scale from 1 "very high perceived task complexity" to 7 "very low perceived task complexity" (Schlereth et al. 2014) and ACA, ASE, and PCPM are rated 6.63 and above on a 9-item scale from 1 "very difficult" to 9 "very easy" (Meißner et al. 2011).

Table 3 gives an overview of the discussed measures. None of the methods shows clear superiority. FastPACE shows weaknesses regarding efficiency. However, none of the methods is assessed as not suitable.

Table 3: Validity, efficiency, and difficulty of the selected methods (Meißner et al. 2011; Netzer and Srinivasan 2011; Schlereth et al. 2014)

Method	Convergent validity	Discriminant validity	Predictive validity	Efficiency	Difficulty
ACA	++	°	°	° | +	° | +
FastPACE			°	-	°
ASE	++	+	° | + | ++	+	° | + | ++
PASE	++	+	+	°	+
PCPM	+	+ | ++	+ | ++	++	+ | ++

4.4.3   Discussion and Evaluation

Studies argue that hybrid methods are most suitable for the class of multi-criteria decision problems considered (e.g. preference measurement in negotiations with incomplete information (Reiser 2013)). Our comparison – without focus on incomplete information but well considering increasing information – cannot support this argument, since ACA as hybrid method and ASE as a self-explicated method both fulfil the requirement of preference adjustment and common validity and efficiency criteria. Moreover, ASE performs better regarding validity and efficiency (Meißner et al. 2011).

The long-standing critique of self-explicated approaches that they do not capture trade-offs (Green and Srinivasan 1990) is addressed by Netzer and Srinivasan (2011). They break down the attribute importance rating into an attribute ranking task followed by pairwise comparisons of attributes, which are appropriate in practical situations (Benítez et al. 2012).

Furthermore, self-explicated approaches are criticised that it is difficult to allocate a constant sum across a large number of attributes. ASE, PASE and PCPM alleviate this problem by ranking the attributes and/or conducting pairwise comparisons, in which the decision maker distributes a constant sum among the two attributes to be compared (Netzer and Srinivasan 2011; Schlereth et al. 2014; Scholz et al. 2010).

Regarding self-explicated approaches, it is argued, that the first stage of self-explicated approaches, in which the desirability of alternatives is rated directly, is perceived as complex and results in high cognitive burden. However, in two-stage self-explicated approaches, irrespectively of the particular method, the first stage is considered to provide reliable results with good predictive power (Schlereth et al. 2014).

Self-explicated approaches are well suited to measure consumer preferences for multi-attribute products that involve many attributes (Netzer and Srinivasan 2011). Since decompositional approaches become taxing with more attributes, which results in higher effort and cognitive burden for the decision maker (Schlereth et al. 2014), self-explicated approaches are currently more popular to estimate preferences for complex products (Schlereth et al. 2014; Scholz et al. 2010).

Regarding the qualitative and the quantitative assessment, we found a self-explicated method to be superior to hybrid methods, namely the ASE approach by Netzer and Srinivasan (2011) (cf. Table 4). In line with our finding, Matzner et al. (2015) choose a self-explicated approach over conjoint analysis for their preference measurement in information systems design choices, because of the superior handling of a large number of attributes, greater usability for respondents, and greater ease in terms of data collection.

Table 4: Overall evaluation of the pre-selected methods. Hy: Hybrid; CA: Conjoint analysis; SE: Self-Explicated

Method	Type	Qualitative assessment		Quantitative assessment		
		Fulfilment of Req4	Possibility to expand	Validity	Efficiency	Difficulty
ACA	Hy	+*)	+	+	° | +	° | +
FastPACE	Hy	+*)	+	°	-	°
CARDS	CA	-	--			
ASE	SE	+*)	++	++	+	+
PASE	SE	+*)	++	++	°	+
PCPM	SE	-	°	++	++	++ | +

4.5   Conclusion and Outlook

Individual interactive preference measurement in a dynamic environment is challenging (Nebro et al. 2018). We evaluated self-explicated approaches – ASE, PASE, and PCPM – a conjoint analysis approach – CARDS – and hybrid approaches – ACA and FastPACE – using a mixed-methods approach. Their suitability for a decision context, in which the decision problem itself may change over time, is both qualitatively (if the methods fulfil the identified requirements respectively if they can be expanded to fulfil them), and quantitatively assessed (validity, efficiency, difficulty). Our result is that none of the methods is suitable in a dynamic environment per se, however, some methods provide inherent mechanisms, which can be reused for preference adjustment processes. ASE, PASE, ACA, and FastPACE provide direct ratings and paired comparisons, which can be repeated. Recalulation of the utility model is required, however, these methods do already update utility values after sets of comparisons. ASE and PASE as self-explicated approaches have the advantage that attribute and value preferences are separated per se (although they are connected because attributes are assessed based on their best and worst cases), which simplifies repetition of single preference questions, while an efficient dynamic extension of ACA and FastPACE is more complex, because the conjoint part builds upon the direct ratings. Hence, repetition of steps of the compositional and the decompositional approach would be necessary, which results in higher effort.

Regarding validity, efficiency, and difficulty of the survey, ASE and PASE are superior to ACA and FastPACE. ASE outperforms PASE in terms of efficiency, because PASE includes an additional step of rating attributes according to their importance. The value of this step, which is intended to reduce the cognitive burden on the decision makers, however, is not great enough to be reflected in the difficulty.

The aim of this study cannot be to provide a holistic study comparing all existing preference measurement methods. We aimed to consider the most appropriate, most promising state-of-the-art methods. However, we cannot ensure that a well-suitable one was missed.

We did not evaluate the performance of the methods by ourselves but referred to empirical studies, which limits the comparability of the empirical results. However, our attempt to remedy this limitation was to involve three different studies to gain a comprehensive picture.

The results of this paper are generalisable to all contexts, in which an individual decision maker must measure preferences for a multiple objective decision problem applying multi-attribute utility theory where the decision problem scope and/or preferences change over time to require the decision maker to interactively adjust his/her preferences. Such circumstances are found in various application domains, e.g. optimising traffic (Nebro et al. 2018) replacements configurations for multi-component systems (Certa et al. 2013), surgical patients' prioritisation (Abbasgholizadeh Rahimi et al. 2016), or decision support in nego-tiations (Kersten et al. 1990), e.g. requirements negotiations (Lenz and Schoop 2017 see chapter 3).

Our results suggest to extend ASE for a dynamic context. As in our intro-ductory example of preference measurement in negotiations, we have developed a dynamic preference adjustment method based on ASE to fit dynamic demands for a negotiation context (chapter 5) and designed dynamic decision support for the case of requirements negotiations (Lenz 2018).

4.6 Acknowledgements

We gratefully acknowledge A. Lenz' PhD grant by the State Baden-Württemberg and the support of the research area "Negotiation Research - Transformation, Technology, Media, and Costs", Faculty of Business, Economics, and Social Sciences at the University of Hohenheim.

5 DynASE – A Method for Dynamic Preference Adjustment in Electronic Negotiations[3]

5.1 Introduction

Negotiations are iterative communication and decision making processes, characterised by their dynamic nature. They are interdependent processes between different parties who seek a joint solution by exchanging information, arguments, and offers (Bichler et al. 2003). In negotiations, a multitude of decisions must be made, e.g. when to start negotiations, with whom to negotiate, which offer to formulate, etc. Electronic media offer an additional value in negotiations by supporting decision making and communication (Schoop 2010). Decision support helps to understand the decision problem, to express preferences, and to formulate, compare, and accept offers (conclude the negotiation process) based on the negotiator's preferences. Thus, we focus on the equally important support of decision making in asynchronous electronic negotiations.

Preference measurement methods used in negotiations are usually one-shot approaches, which assume a static context. However, negotiations are reciprocal processes as the negotiators' behaviour affects the shape of the negotiation itself. For example, during the process the negotiators expand, narrow, or alter the negotiation space (cf. agenda negotiations; Fernandes 2016), which requires new preferences to be elicited or existing preferences to be adjusted. Furthermore, an increase of the information level during the negotiation process may result in preference changes (Reiser and Schoop 2012). Alternatively, the process dynamics (Curhan et al. 2004; Vetschera 2007) require negotiators to adjust their preferences. Due to the dynamic environment, the decision problem itself, its attributes, alternatives, and/or preference information may change. Outdated and/or missing preference information decreases the effectivity of electronic decision support in negotiations. Thus, the need for dynamic preference measurement methods, which take the dimension of time into account to handle changes, becomes clear. Dynamic preference measurement is extremely complex (Nebro et al. 2018). Initial methods adapted for a dynamic negotiation context exist, e.g. focusing on process dynamics taking imprecise preference information

---

3   Co-Author: Prof. Mareike Schoop, PhD.

into account (Reiser 2013; Roszkowska and Wachowicz 2015a) or learning a negotiator's preference structures (Guo et al. 2003). However, helping decision makers to fine-tune their preferences in an environment where the decision context itself changes over time is challenging, especially when a high number of objectives is involved (Nebro et al. 2018), which is why literature on dynamic, interactive approaches for an individual negotiator is still scarce (Reiser et al. 2012; Reiser 2013).

Our aim is to enable dynamic preference adjustment during the electronic negotiation process, which efficiently handles preference adjustment due to changes in the scope of the decision problem (i.e. adding, withdrawing, modifying issues and/or alternatives) and preference adjustment due to information increase or process dynamics without agenda changes. Preference measurement must be possible for an individual negotiator. The method must allow interactivity (cf. Nebro et al. 2018), to allow the negotiators to redefine their preferences according to an increasing knowledge during the negotiation process.

For negotiations, preference measurement methods are mainly derived from multi-criteria decision analysis and adapted to negotiation specifics (Almeida and Wachowicz 2017). We choose one multi-criteria preference measurement method, which is well-suitable to be extended to address the above illustrated use cases. To do so, we choose the Adaptive Self-Explication (ASE) approach, since it has more potential for dynamic extension than other state-of-the-art methods (for a discussion see Lenz and Schoop 2019 in chapter 4) and performs well in terms of validity, efficiency, and survey task complexity (Lenz and Schoop 2019; Meißner et al. 2011; Netzer and Srinivasan 2011; Schlereth et al. 2014). The focus of the present paper is on the expansion of the ASE to address the use cases efficiently leading to preference adjustment. We evaluate the novel method empirically in a laboratory experiment complemented by a survey.

To this end, the remainder of the paper is structured as follows. In chapter 5.2, suitable multi-criteria decision analysis methods and the choice for ASE are discussed briefly. ASE is described in detail and relevant use cases of preference adjustment are presented. In chapter 5.3 the dynamic extension of ASE is developed, while chapter 5.4 describes its implementation in a negotiation support system. In chapter 5.5, an empirical study is discussed, which demonstrates the applicability of the dynamic method and its superiority in terms of efficiency over a static alternative. Chapter 5.6 discusses our approach and findings. Chapter 5.7 concludes the paper and gives a brief outlook.

5.2 Preference Measurement in Electronic Negotiations

5.2.1 Multi-Attribute Utility Theory and Assumptions Made

A multitude of multi-criteria decision analysis methods exists to assess alternatives of a decision problem. The spectrum of methods comprises of outranking methods (e.g. the ELECTRE family (Roy 1990) or PROMETHEE family (Brans and Vincke 1985)), fuzzy methods (Chen and Hwang 1992), robust ordinal regression methods (Greco et al. 2008), or UTA methods (Jacquet-Lagreze and Siskos 1982). Decision support in electronic negotiations commonly utilises multi-attribute utility theory (Keeney and Raiffa 1976) to formulate a linear-additive utility function to assess an offer comprising of a chosen set of negotiation alternatives of the form

$$U(A) = \sum_i w_i * u(x_i) \tag{2}$$

with utility u of alternative x of the i th issue weighted by the issue's relative importance w_i. Utility is a hypothetical, empirically non-observable assessment measure, which allows the comparison of negotiation alternatives (Voeth et al. 2007).

To assign utilities, the decision maker's preferences must to be extracted. These are subject to the assumptions of preferential consistency, transitivity, and independence (cf. Luce and Raiffa 1957). In order to be able to solve the decision problem, it is decomposed into the decision between two alternatives depending on the preference measurement method. This means that preferences for two alternatives each are elicited. This results in a set of preferences relations for the alternatives. It is assumed that this set of preference relations satisfies a certain consistency. A constraint for some rules of composition of the preferences effects an overall consistency so that utilities can be assigned to the alternatives. Preferential transitivity holds between any alternatives. If alternative A is preferred over alternative B and alternative B is preferred over alternative C, then A is preferred over C. This implies also, that the alternatives must be comparable. Furthermore, preferential independence of the negotiation alternatives is assumed. Alternatives influencing each other must be reformulated, aggregated or decomposed in advance.

5.2.2 Approaches

Most current negotiation support systems provide different static preference measurement methods from which the negotiator can choose. These static methods can roughly be categorised into approaches of direct preference measurement (compositional approaches), conjoint measurement (decompositional approaches), or hybrid approaches (Voeth et al. 2007). For example, direct preference measurement is provided by eAgora (Chen et al. 2005), Inspire (Kersten and Noronha 1999b), NeGoGo (Lai et al. 2007), Negoisst (Schoop 2010), and WebNS (Yuan 2003). NegoManage (Brzostowski and Wachowicz 2014) and SmartSettle (Thiessen and Soberg 2003) build on conjoint measurement. Hybrid approaches are applied in Inspire and Negoisst. Whilst these represent static approaches implemented in negotiation support systems, eAgora, Inspire, Negoisst and SmartSettle additionally enable preference changes providing functionalities which allow subsequent direct complementation in the case of new issues and/or modification of preferences.

Various approaches have been developed which focus on the dynamic aspect of measuring preferences. Abbasgholizadeh Rahimi et al. (2016) propose a three-step framework to define the prioritisation of surgical patients. They build their framework on fuzzy logic, using the Analytic Hierarchy Process (Saaty 1990) to gain the stakeholders' objectives. The patients' condition is assessed to get a prioritisation of the patients. Lastly, dynamic aspects are considered, i.e. the patients' health condition. Opinions of both the surgery team members and the patients are integrated. The decision problem changes by adding or deleting patients. Transferred to the negotiation context, new negotiation offers are assessed during the negotiation process, which is realised by decision support. However, the objectives and importance weightings (which correspond to negotiation issues and their importance weights) do not change dynamically. Thus, Abbasgholizadeh Rahimi et al. (2016) consider different types of changes regarding preference measurement.

Li et al. (2015) propose a model for dynamic fuzzy multi-criteria decision making. They integrate both the decision maker's preferences and what they call "objective" information. In negotiations, objective information is also gathered in the preparation phase. However, information on negotiation issues and their values is assessed by the negotiator. Their focus is on modelling dynamic preferences instead of the measurement itself. Benítez et al. (2012) focus on ensuring the mathematical consistency of preference information gained by pairwise comparisons. They do not propose a method for eliciting preferences either. Both focus on the mathematical model, whilst our focus is on an electronic dynamic measurement of preferences during negotiations.

The approaches of Certa et al. (2013) and Nebro et al. (2018) aim to solve an optimisation problem by finding the best suitable solution. For decision support in negotiations, we intend to apply a utility based method, which allows the assessment of all alternatives (Keeney and Raiffa 1976; Raiffa et al. 2002).

Newer approaches for preference measurement in electronic negotiations consider process dynamics and take a processual view, e.g. they assume uncertain information at the beginning of a negotiation, conduct an ex post preference measurement at an increased information level (Reiser 2013), or handle ill-structured negotiation problems throughout the process (Roszkowska and Wachowicz 2015a). Reiser (2013) proposes a two-part approach to consider incomplete and uncertain information, in which, however, the scope of the decision problem remains the same throughout the process, whilst Roszkowska and Wachowicz (2015a) do not consider preference changes.

Our aim is to provide processual preference adjustment to contribute in the area of dynamic preference measurement in electronic negotiations. In particular, adjusting preference measurement at any time taking all information known at the time into consideration is enabled. To address changes causing the need for adjusting preference measurement in a systematic way, we derive the following types based on existing literature.

The negotiation agenda comprises of the issues and their values to be negotiated. Their specific combination is of importance for the success of a negotiation (Fernandes 2016). This negotiation agenda is not stable throughout the negotiation, but underlies change (Pendergast 1990). During an ongoing negotiation, the negotiation parties communicate their information, interests, and preferences, which impacts the negotiation agenda itself (Pendergast 1990). Changes of the agenda may play a pivotal role in reaching a joint, mutually beneficial negotiation solution (Fernandes 2016). Introducing additional issues and values during the negotiation as well as dropping negotiation issues which are no longer important for the negotiation will require changes in the preference structure: "Newly identified issues are added, issues are revised and unnecessary issues are dropped." (Fernandes 2016, p. 19). Based on such agenda changes, we derive the cases of (A) a new issue, (B) a new value without a new issue, (D) deleted issue value, and (F) deleted issue.

Even without explicit changes of the negotiation agenda, a negotiator's preferences may change during an ongoing negotiation (Ausubel et al. 2002; Reiser 2013). The longer a negotiation continues, the more information is exchanged which will affect their preferences (Reiser and Schoop 2012). Moreover, the dynamics of the negotiation process itself (e.g. reciprocal interaction of the negotiators) have an impact on the negotiators' preferences (Curhan et al. 2004; Vetschera 2007). Thus, we consider the cases of (C) changed value preference information and (E) changed issue preference information in our approach.

Lenz and Schoop (2019, see chapter 4) assess six state-of-the-art and/or popular mainly adaptive preference measurement methods regarding their suitability for dynamic extension. These methods are three direct preference measurement methods, namely the ASE (Netzer and Srinivasan 2011), the Pre-Sorted Adaptive Self-Explication (Schlereth et al. 2014), and the Pairwise Comparison-based Preference Measurement (Scholz et al. 2010); one indirect preference measurement method, namely the Conjoint Adaptive Ranking Database System (Dahan et al. 2004); and two hybrid preference measurement methods, namely the Adaptive Conjoint Analysis (Johnson 1987) (which is the predominant approach in this field (Herbst and Voeth 2015)) and the Fast Polyhedral Adaptive Conjoint Estimation (Toubia et al. 2003) which builds on the Adaptive Conjoint Analysis. Lenz and Schoop (2019, see chapter 4) argue that ASE is superior compared to the other methods referring to the possibility to extend it for dynamic means, mainly derived by ASE's strength to require minimal preference information depending on other attributes/values. Moreover, it performs well regarding its efficiency, shows high validity and low complexity.

ASE is a compositional preference measurement approach with adaptive question design (Netzer and Srinivasan 2011). It is designed to solve the self-explicated constant sum question problem when the number of product attributes becomes large (Netzer and Srinivasan 2011). The ASE assumes preferential independence of attributes and values. In the first stage, the desirability of all issue values is directly rated for each issue. In the second stage, the relative importance across the issues is assessed in two steps. Firstly, the decision maker ranks all issues based on their worst case and their best case. Secondly, there is a pairwise comparison of issues. Hereby, the paired comparisons are provided in an adaptive manner, aiming at comparisons which provide the most information. In the pairwise comparison, a constant sum of 100 points is divided for the two issues. After each set of comparisons, a log-linear multiple regression is performed to estimate the issue weightings and to choose the next comparison to be asked. There are three potential termination conditions: a preset number of paired comparisons is reached; the regression error is smaller than a predefined level; or all issues are compared at least once.

5.2.3 Perception of the Preference Measurement Method and Its Results

Although the main goal of the method to be designed is progress in terms of efficiency, research postulates that the user perception is important for its acceptance, its actual usage and thus for its success and value. In the literature, these perception criteria are not clearly to be considered or clearly irrelevant. We follow different lines of argumentation. By means of the perception measures, we combine the research stream of Information Systems and research in preference measurement. "Computer systems cannot improve organizational performance if they aren't used" (Davis et al. 1989, p. 982). The technology acceptance model (Davis et al. 1989) is an established model in Information Systems research to predict the adoption behaviour of users. Two key determinants for a user's attitude towards using a system are the perceived usefulness and the perceived ease of use. According to Dabholkar (1994), fun is one of the "meaningful expectancy-value component[s]" (p. 109) "for the adoption of computer software packages" (Dabholkar 1994, p. 119). Matzner et al. (2015) also address this construct, measuring ease of use adapted from Dabholkar (1994). Again, this is supported by Gerow et al. (2013): Intrinsic motivation factors such as perceived enjoyment are relevant for predicting use intentions of utilitarian systems. Correspondingly, in preference measurement research, the user's enjoyment influences the user's acceptance. Netzer and Srinivasan (2011, p. 152) "asked respondents for feedback about their experience with the preference measurement task. Specifically, [...] the difficulty and clarity of the task, the degree of enjoyment derived from completing the task, and their personal assessment of how well the survey was able to capture their preferences." Meißner et al. (2011) also ask for the overall liking of the survey. Existing criteria must be applied to assess the performance of the method developed. Thus, in addition to the objectively measured efficiency, the user's perception of the efficiency of the method, which we aim for, is to be assessed. In addition, aside from the objective accuracy of the preferences, the user's perceived accuracy and fun must be considered to avoid shortcomings of the method.

5.3 Extension of ASE to Fit Dynamic Demands

In an initial preference elicitation, all knowledge at the time is considered. The initial preference elicitation is adapted from Netzer and Srinivasan's (2011) ASE. The user dialogue comprises of three steps, namely (1) rating of issue values for each issue, (2) ranking of issues according to their importance, (3) pairwise comparisons of issues. In the following, we describe the ASE (Netzer and Srinivasan 2011) transferred to negotiation issues and negotiation values (cf. Figure 7).

1) **Rating of issue values** (user dialogue): In stage 1, one issue i at a time is presented to the user who is then asked to rate the best case and worst case for the issue as well as intermediate values x_i on an 11-point scale from 0 to 100 in steps of ten. The step is repeated until values of all issues are rated to obtain the utility of all values of all issues $u(x)_i$.

2) **Ranking of issues** (user dialogue): In stage 2, a list of all issues is presented to the user. The user must rank all issues according to importance to obtain their rank r_i . To get meaningful results, the improvement of the worst case to the best case of each issue is presented as well.

3) **Select initial paired comparisons** (backend): Based on the ranking, three initial paired comparisons are identified, which are sequentially presented to the user. The first comparison comprises of the issue ranked best $r_i = 1$ and the issue ranked worst $r_i = R$ with $R = Number\ of\ issues$. The second

comparison comprises of the issue ranked best $r_i = 1$ and the issue ranked in

the middle $r_i = \begin{cases} \frac{R}{2} & , if\, R\ is\ even \\ \frac{R+1}{2} & , if\ R\ is\ odd \end{cases}$. The third comparison comprises of the

issue ranked middle and the issue ranked worst.

4) **Pairwise comparison of issues** (user dialogue): In this step, the user compares the relative importance of two issues i_1 and i_2 to obtain their ratio $v_{i_1 i_2}$.

5) **Estimation of issue importance weights** (backend): A log-linear regression is performed based on all issue comparison ratios $v_{i_1 i_2}$, which have been obtained at this point, to estimate importance weights e_i of the compared issues.

6) **Interpolation of remaining issues** (backend): The estimated importance weights e_i are used to interpolate the importance weights l_i of the remaining issues linearly between two estimated importance weights. The issues are interpolated according to their rank. The first issue, whose importance weight is interpolated, is the first issue ranked after an issue, whose importance is estimated $i_{r_{e_{i_{first}}}+1}$. Its importance weight is linearly interpolated based on the estimated importance weight of the first issue of the interval $e_{i_{first}}$, the estimated importance weight of the last issue of the interval $e_{i_{last}}$, the number of issues within the interval N, and the rank of the issue in the interval:

$$l_{i_{r_{e_{i_{first}}}+n}} = e_{i_{first}} - \frac{e_{i_{first}} - e_{i_{last}}}{N+1} * n \tag{3}$$

7) **Normalisation of issue importance weights** (backend): The estimated weights e_i of all issues, which have been compared at least once, and the interpolated weights l_i of all issues, which have not been compared yet, are normalised to obtain relative importance w_i so that $\sum_i w_i = 100$.

8) **Check termination criteria** (backend): Having the value ratings $u(x_i)$ of stage 1 and relative issue importance weights w_i of stage 2, a first tentative linear additive utility model is obtained. This way, an initial preference measurement can be performed very fast to quickly gain preference information to use in the negotiation. Three termination criteria are checked. If a pre-defined number of paired comparisons is reached, or if a pre-defined error of the log-linear regression is reached, or if all issues are compared at least once, the preference measurement is terminated. If the preference information is not yet sufficient, stage 2 is entered again and further paired comparisons are conducted.

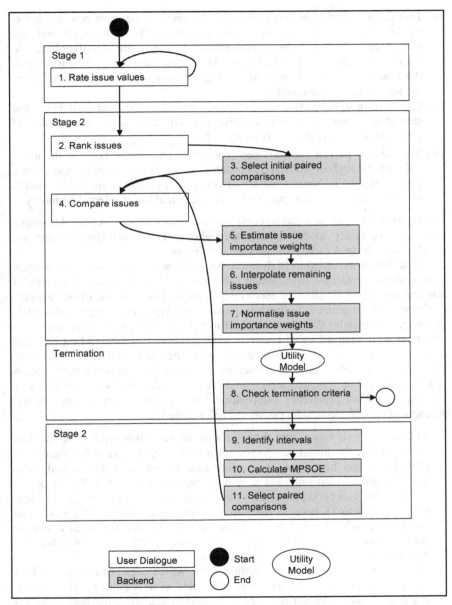

Figure 7: Initial preference elicitatioin process adapted from Netzer and Srinivasan (2011)

9) **Identification of intervals** (backend): To provide the most possible information, pairwise comparisons are selected adaptively. To do so, intervals between the issues, which have been compared already, are identified based on their relative importance weights w_i. As a result, intervals o, their issue with the lowest rank, their issue with the highest rank, and the number of intermediate issues m are identified.

10) **Calculation of MPSOE** (backend): The interval with the maximum possible sum of interpolation errors (MPSOE) is identified. To do so, the MPSOE of each interval is calculated. $MPSOE_o = (w_{i_{highest}} - w_{i_{lowest}}) * m/2$.

11) **Selection of paired comparisons** (backend): The middle issue of the interval with the highest MPSOE is chosen to generate new paired comparisons. From this middle issue, a bundle of two paired comparisons is determined, in which the issue is compared with the upper and lower interval boundary.

Having identified two new paired comparisons, steps 4 to 7 are repeated to gain a new tentative utility model as described above. The termination criteria are checked (step 8) to decide, if the process terminates.

The ASE is extended to fit dynamic demands as follows. The major concept is to keep all preference information, which is valid at the time. This includes information gained by all three user dialogue steps. This way, the effort to adjust preferences is minimised. Following the different types of change of the environment, we consider the cases of (A) a new issue, (B) a new value without a new issue, (C) changed value preference information, (D) deleted best or worst case (implies a new best or worst case deleting the old one), (E) changed issue preference information, and (F) deleted issue. The preference adjustment process is very lean and an adjusted utility model can be calculated very quickly. Depending on which preference information has changed, different steps of the adjustment process need to be performed (cf. Figure 8).

A) In case of a new issue, only the values of the new issue have to be rated as performed in the initial preference elicitation (step 1). All value ratings of other issues and the existing issue ranking can be reused. It is presented to the decision maker who only has to sort in the new issue (step 2). All paired comparisons can be kept. At this point, a utility model can already be calculated (steps 5 to 7), because the relative importance weight of the new issue can be interpolated based on the issue ranking. The usual criteria terminate the adjustment process (step 8), i.e. two paired comparisons including the new issue can be performed if desired (step 4).

B) If a new value is added to an existing issue, which does not replace the best or worst case of the respective issue, it is rated as in A (step 1). The remaining process steps are not required to be performed, since the preference information for all other decision elements remain the same. The partial utility value of the newly rated value is included in the utility model.

C) If the preference information of an existing issue value has changed, the preference adjustment process is the same as in B (step 1). The respective issue and its value ratings is presented to the decision maker, who corrects the respective value.

D) If the best or worst case of an issue is deleted or its preference has changed as there is a new best or worst case for the issue (step 1), this affects also the issue ranking and the paired comparisons (steps 2 and 4) as in both steps preferences are measured referring to the improvement in the respective issue from worst case to best case, since the assessment of the improvement may change if best or worst case change.

E) In case the preference information for an issue changes, the issue ranking must be checked and corrected (step 2) and all related paired comparisons must be adjusted (step 3). Based thereon, the utility model can be recalculated (steps 5 to 7).

F) If an issue is deleted, the decision maker does not need to adjust preferences as long as other preference information is not affected. The issue is deleted from the agenda itself as well as from the ranking. The utility model is recalculated disregarding related paired comparisons (steps 5 to 7).

Although all types of changes have been described individually, it is possible to deal with several changes of different types and/or of the same type in the same preference adjustment process simultaneously.

Key elements and resulting strengths of the dynamic preference adjustment process developed are the following. Separation of preference information and utility model enables adaptive selection of paired comparisons to reduce effort for the decision maker as provided by ASE (Netzer and Srinivasan 2011).

When the negotiation agenda can be decomposed into non-overlapping subgroups, for which independent utility functions can be formulated, separable preferences exist (cf. Voeth 2000). If so, keeping track of preference information to update outdated preferences (add, delete, modify), enables to keep the effort required for the decision maker at a minimum. This way, the new dimension of time is introduced. A repetition of steps (Certa et al. 2013) allows the articulation of new preference information.

The preference adjustment process can be triggered at the decision maker's convenience (Benítez et al. 2012; Nebro et al. 2018). It is an interactive approach (Benítez et al. 2012; Nebro et al. 2018).

One major advantage is that it does not matter how many or which issues have been compared. Each comparison is considered as an observation of the underlying preference function. The regression analysis obtaining this preference

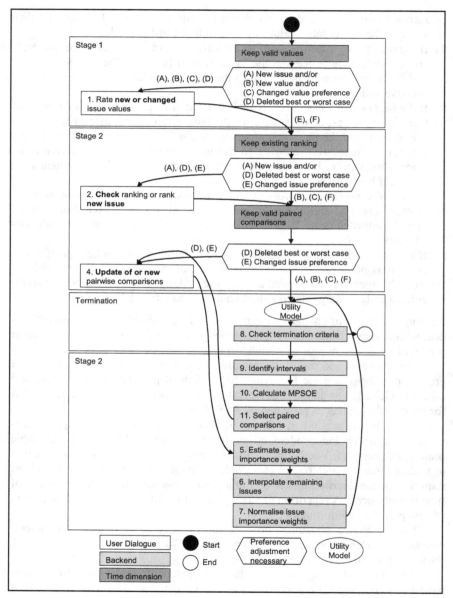

Figure 8:   Preference adjustment process with time-dependent dynamic extension based on Netzer and Srinivasan (2011)

function can handle unbalanced information in contrast to methods, where symmetrical matrices play an important role. The consistency measure of the regression analysis can be obtained. (Netzer and Srinivasan 2011)

Moreover, separation of preference information collection for values and issues reduces complexity and the scope of how much preference information must be adjusted in case of changes. Nevertheless, preferences for values and issues are connected by a comparisons of the improvement in an issue from its worst case to its best case to avoid detached preference information.

At any time after the three initial paired comparisons, relative importance weightings for all issues are available. Thus, a first tentative utility model can be retained very quickly, which allows quick assessment of offers. The second stage can be interrupted for this purpose, but may also be entered again, if a more precise utility model is desired.

Another advantage is that in the case of a new issue, no paired comparison must be conducted at all. The relative importance weight for the issue can be linearly interpolated based on the issue ranking.

Similar to Nebro et al. (2018), the preference adjustment approach developed can handle changes in both the decision problem and the preference information. The decision makers can initiate changes at any moment. Especially in dyadic processes, where new information is gathered externally and preference information evolves, it is important that the decision makers can actively interact with the method, iteratively seeking information and fine-tuning their preference information (Nebro et al. 2018).

To this end, preferences can be derived already on the basis of a small amount of information. Available information at the beginning is sufficient to build a tentative utility model. These preference adjustment steps can be repeated as many times as necessary. Gradually, the preference information will be completed eventually. (Benítez et al. 2012)

5.4 Implementation of DynASE

DynASE can be implemented in any negotiation support system or decision support system, which uses a linear-additive utility model to support decision making, without any media discontinuity. We implemented DynASE in the negotiation support system Negoisst (Schoop et al. 2003). Negoisst is an asynchronous web-based negotiation support system, which follows an integrated approach providing decision support, communication support, and document management (Schoop et al. 2003; Schoop 2010). Negoisst's extensive analytical features for decision support (cf. Reiser 2013) are based on the negotiators'

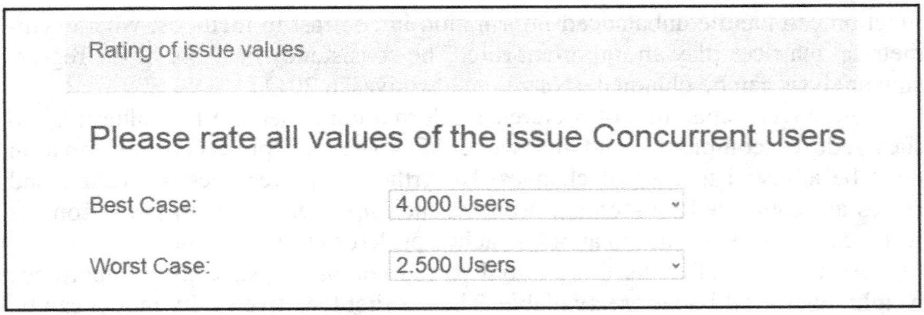

Figure 9:   Rating of issue values (step 1)

explicated preferences on the negotiation issues and values. The negotiators exchange semi-structured messages, comprising of unstructured, enriched text along with structured, formal offers (Köhne et al. 2005; Schoop 2005; Schoop et al. 2014). Based on their explicated preferences, these offers are quantified using concepts of multi-attribute utility theory (Keeney and Raiffa 1976), and thus made comparable. Moreover, the negotiators are visually supported in their tasks by a history graph (Gettinger et al. 2012), which displays the development of the utility values of offers over time and thus provides information on the negotiators' convergence during the negotiation process, allowing the negotiators to analyse their concessions and gains.

For the use case of (A) adding a new issue, which will be the example of our empirical study, the following user dialogue interactions are required. Figures 9 to 11 depict their implementation in Negoisst. Figure 9 shows the rating of values of an issue (step 1). In the example, values of the issue 'concurrent users' are rated. Since this is a numeric issue, for which integer values between 2,500 users and 4,000 users are possible in the upcoming negotiation, the negotiator only rates which interval boundary is the worst case and which one is the best case. As we assume a linear partial utility function, values in between can be calculated in the backend. For categorical issues, the values for best and worst case are also elicited. However, additional values must be rated on a scale from 0 to 100 in intervals of ten.

Subsequently, all issues are ranked according to their importance (step 2), see Figure 10. As reference point, each issue's worst case and best case are depicted.

To refine the issue weightings, issues are compared pairwise in the subsequent interaction step (step 4). The ratio of the issue weightings can be entered via a slider or via input fields beneath the slider, see Figure 11. In each case, the resulting ratio is depicted. Again, the respective issues' improvement from worst

Please rank the following improvements of issues by dragging and dropping order.

Ranking an issue does not imply a change in any best case, worst case, or other value.

Most important

Worst case → Best Case

≡ **Standalone or integration**   Standalone → Integration

≡ **Concurrent users**   2,500 Users → 4,000 Users

≡ **Registration**   ITL accounts → University accounts and guest accounts

≡ **Product name**   ITL → GeSCo

≡ **Interfaces**   Manual slides import → Automated slides import and data export

≡ **Brainstorming**   No transformation → Transformation into survey

Least important

Worst case → Best Case

Figure 10:   Ranking of issues (step 2)

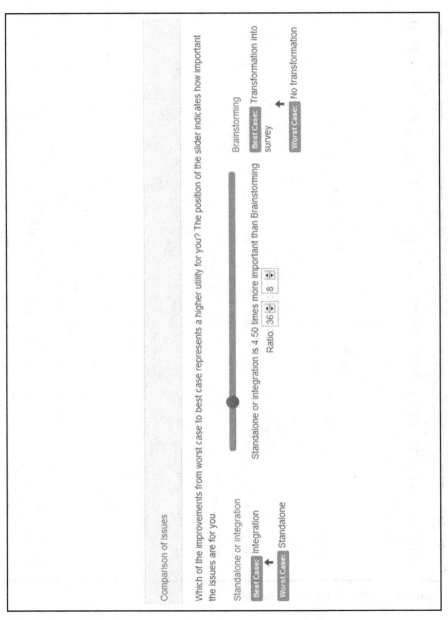

Figure 11:   Pairwise comparison (step 4)

to best case are depicted to support the negotiator to get a better understanding of the range of the issues.

Thereafter, an initial preference elicitation is completed and the negotiators can view their resulting preferences. In use case A, during the negotiation process, an additional issue is put on the negotiation table. The negotiators then may adjust their preferences with respect to the new issue. In this case, DynASE repeats the first step for the new issue to rate the values of the new issue (cf. Figure 9). Subsequently, the existing ranking is shown and the negotiator is requested to insert the new issue into the ranking. After the adjustment of the issue ranking, the adjusted issue weightings can be calculated using interpolation for the new issue. However, for refined issue weightings, pairwise comparisons for the new issue may be conducted as in Figure 11.

5.5   Empirical Study

The aim of the empirical study is to evaluate the newly developed DynASE. An evaluation of interactive dynamic preference measurement methods in negotiations is difficult (cf. Danielson and Ekenberg 2016, Helbig et al. 2016) since there is a lack of standardised evaluation approaches. Firstly, an adequate comparable method needs to be found. Secondly, adequate evaluation criteria for dynamic preference measurement in electronic negotiations are required.

5.5.1   Comparable Method

We use three mechanisms to evaluate the newly developed method. Firstly, we refer to a given set of preferences, which is common in electronic negotiation research (e.g. Kersten et al. 2017; Vetschera et al. 2006; Vetschera 2007). Secondly, we evaluate DynASE empirically simulating one use case. To do so, we choose the use case of A, which is to add an issue to the negotiation agenda after preference measurement has been completed, since this use case is considered to be one of the most complex, sophisticated, and challenging use cases (cf. Benítez et al. 2012) as an attribute is added to the existing decision problem, which affects the relative weighting of all existing attributes. Thirdly, we use a static alternative of DynASE, which could realistically be applied if there was no dynamic extension. Participants using the static alternative serve as the control group in our design. The ASE is used as the static alternative to mitigate disruptive factors, e.g. the type and design of survey tasks of different methods. However, the ASE captures only snapshots of preferences and is thus not applicable in its present form. For the laboratory simulation, we have modified it using its

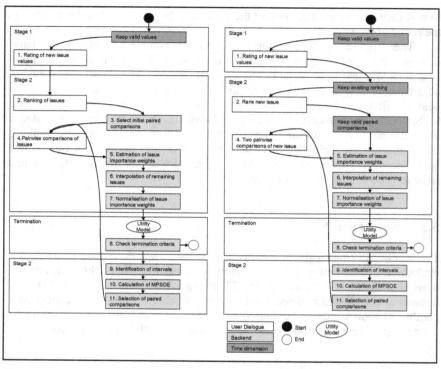

Figure 12:   Static (left) and dynamic (right) preference adjustment in case of a new issue

existing mechanisms and reusing its three user dialogue steps. For the use case A, this means, that the rating of issue values (step 1) is not repeated in total during the preference adjustment. Only the values of the new issue are rated to make it comparable to DynASE. The remaining two user dialogue steps (steps 2 and 4) are repeated as usual by ASE. Since both the static and the dynamic method build on the same preference measurement method, we can relate observed differences directly back to the different adjustment process.

We have ensured that the above described use case can be performed by both preference measurement alternatives. In the static method, the preference measurement is partially repeated to capture the new attribute. The static and dynamic preference adjustment processes differ for the case of a new requirement in the ranking of issues (step 2), the comparisons of issues (step 4), and in the initiating of the calculation of a (tentative) utility model, see Figure 12. Whilst the ranking of the issues (step 2) must be repeated in the static alternative, the existing issue ranking is presented to the user in the dynamic alternative, who sorts the new issue in and checks the remaining ranking. Subsequently, the static alternative requires issue comparisons (step 4), the dynamic preference adjustment can already calculate a (tentative) utility model based on the issue ranking and valid issue comparisons from the initial preference elicitation (steps 5 to 7). The dynamic preference adjustment refines this utility model by conducting two comparisons for the new issue (step 4). As a result, the static preference adjustment requires eleven issue comparisons, the dynamic preference adjustment requires two issue comparisons to get a precise utility model for the negotiation case applied.

We only assess results of the preference adjustment process, not the prior preference elicitation process to capture the specifics of dynamic preference measurement.

5.5.2 Procedure and Participants

We conducted a negotiation simulation, which covers the pre-negotiation phase, complemented by a post-questionnaire. The negotiation case newly developed for this study represents a requirements negotiation between a student committee represented by one member – the focal negotiator – and a software vendor negotiating requirements for an audience response system to be developed on the basis of the negotiated agreement (see appendix A1). The agenda comprises of three types of issues in requirements negotiations, namely two design related issues, three technology related issues, and two contract related issues. All participants are asked to adopt the role of the student committee member to ensure comparability of their preference measurement.

The participants were briefed by one of the authors. The briefing covered a demonstration of preference measurement in Negoisst (without preference adjustment as to not disclose the two variants) and giving an overview of the negotiation case. Afterwards, the participants had to elicit their preferences initially based on the negotiation case within three days (see appendix A1). After the preference elicitation, a new issue was centrally deployed in Negoisst (agenda change) with the relevant new preference information (see appendix A2). Subsequently the participants had to adjust their preferences either dynamically or statically. A post-questionnaire complements the data by the students' demographics and subjective perceptions. As an incentive, the students received a score for their final course grade.

Our research design represents a 2x1 between-subject-design, since all participants occupied the same negotiation role, namely the role of the student committee member. The participants were assigned to groups for dynamic preference adjustment and static preference adjustment.

Table 5: Research design

	Dynamic preference adjustment	Static preference adjustment
(A) New issue	42	39

The participants comprised of graduate students, who were trained in negotiation. We ensured their negotiation and English skills (cf. Lai et al. 2010). An electronic negotiation simulation was conducted in January 2018 with 81 participants at a German University. The majority of the participants was German (66.7 %). Other participants were Spanish (9.9%), Bangladeshi (3.7 %), Bulgarian (2.5 %), Ukrainian (2.5%) Chinese, Italian, Mexican, Moldovan, Nepalese, Russian, Swiss, Vietnamese (all 1.3%). One participant did not disclose their nationality. The students were assigned prior to one of the two groups, having static preference adjustment (39 participants, 48.1%) or dynamic preference adjustment (42 participants, 51.9%), see Table 5.

5.5.3 Measures

As described above, it is difficult to assess the validity of a dynamic preference measurement method in electronic negotiations (cf. Danielson and Ekenberg 2016). We aim to ensure the accuracy of the preference adjustment process and its efficiency in terms of its duration.

We evaluate the accuracy of the developed method by an objective assessment of the resulting utility model compared to the given preferences (cf. Roszkowska and Wachowicz 2015b), subsequently called cardinal inaccuracy. Cardinal inaccuracy is measured by the imprecision error of the utility model, namely the distance of the measured issue weightings to the given issue weightings II and the discrepancy of the value preferences VI_i. The issue inaccuracy II is measured by the sum of the discrepancy of the given issue weighting u_i^{ref} and the participant's issue weighting u_i for all issues i:

$$II = \sum_i |u_i^{ref} - u_i| \tag{4}$$

The implementation of DynASE requires the participant to assign a best and worst case for each issue. Since Roszkowska and Wachowicz (2015b) measure value inaccuracy by the difference of the participant's value rating to the given value rating, a wrong assignment (worst case as best case and best case as worst case) would depend on the actual value of worst case and best case respectively, thus the 'same' value inaccuracy (if best and worst cases are mixed up) of different issues would be assessed differently and the value inaccuracy would be distorted. Hence, we adapt the measurement of the value inaccuracy by Roszkowska and Wachowicz (2015b) to the specifics of the implementation of DynASE and measure the value inaccuracy VI_i based on the number of values of an issue e_i, whose utility is incorrect referring to the given value utility, in relation to the number of values of the respective issue n_i, weighted by the given utility u_i^{ref} for the respective issue:

$$VI_i = u_i^{ref} * \frac{e_i}{n_i} \qquad (5)$$

The cardinal inaccuracy CI is calculated by the sum of the participant's issue inaccuracy II and the value inaccuracy VI_i of all issues eventually:

$$CI = II + \sum_i VI_i \qquad (6)$$

Regarding validity, we assess construct validity, for which convergent validity is adequate for preference measurement in electronic negotiations (Reiser 2013). Convergent validity can be assessed by the correlation of the mean of the issue weightings of the participants of the respective treatment; comparing the ranking of the most important issues per treatment; or top three and bottom three issues; or the spread of the issue weightings and spread of the path worths (Meißner et al. 2011; Schlereth et al. 2014; Scholz et al. 2010). Discriminant validity is measured by the range between the most and least important issues per treatment (Schlereth et al. 2014).

Efficiency is operationalised by the participant's objective duration of conducting the preference adjustment (either static or dynamic), which was automatically tracked by Negoisst.

5.5.4   Descriptive Results

Data cleansing led to a data set of 74 participants. The initial preference elicitation process, which was exactly the same for both treatments, resulted in 62 participants (83.8 %), who elicited exactly the given preferences, see Table 6. We only consider these participants to ensure comparability of the subsequent dynamic respectively static preference adjustment process. 31 participants were female, 31 participants male; average age was 23.8 years (SD = 2.01). Language self-efficacy, negotiation self-efficacy (Lai et al. 2010), and digital media usage were assessed. Daily use of digital media was reported to be very high (2 – 4 hours: 14.5 %, 4 – 6 hours: 29.0 %, 6 – 8 hours: 37.1 %, more than 8 hours: 19.4 %) with a high frequency of usage several times a day (95.2 %). Participants reported well-above negotiation skills (M = 4.58, SD = 1.32) on a 7-point-Likert scale.

Table 6: Issue inaccuracy, value inaccuracy and cardinal inaccuracy of the initial preference elicitation

	Issue Inaccuracy	Value Inaccuracy	Cardinal Inaccuracy
Frequency of correct preferences absolute	66	69	62
Frequency of correct preferences in percent	89.2	93.2	83.8
Mean	1.30	1.01	2.31
Minimum	0.00	0.00	0.00
Maximum	65.00	26.00	89.67

The amount of time required reached from 56 seconds to 1 hour, 30 minutes and 23 seconds (M = 8.82 mins, SD = 16.08). The cardinal inaccuracy was 0 for all participants, which means that all participants adjusted their preferences according to the given preferences.

Regarding validity, cardinal inaccuracy showed that all participants achieved the given utility model. Thus, we assume both very high convergent validity and discriminant validity for both preference adjustment processes. This result is linked to the data cleansing since all participants who did not initially elicit their preferences correctly were eliminated. Unfortunately, we cannot assess convergent validity and discriminant validity of the initial preference elicitation process due to a lack of a comparable treatment group. Nonetheless, this means that both preference adjustment processes show high construct validity, since all remaining participants adjusted their preferences according to the given preferences.

5.5.5 Results

Regarding efficiency, in the mean, participants with static preference adjustment required 12.01 minutes (SD = 19.58) and participants with dynamic preference adjustment required 6.01 minutes (SD = 11.82), see Table 7. A Mann-Whitney U Test was performed. Participants who used the dynamic preference adjustment require highly significant shorter time (Mdn = 3.44 min) than participants who used the static preference adjustment (Mdn = 6.21 min), $U = 166$, $z = 4.41$, $p < .001$, $r = .56$, showing a large effect, cf. Table 8.

Table 7: Descriptives for static and dynamic preference adjustment

	Static adjustment	Dynamic adjustment
N	29 participants	33 participants
Mean	12.01 min	6.00 min
Median	6.21 min	3.44 min
Std. deviation	19.58 min	11.82 min
Minimum	3.38 min	0.94 min
Maximum	100.39 min	70.51 min

The objective cardinal inaccuracy is measured using (6). Surprisingly, all participants achieved a cardinal inaccuracy of 0, which means that none of them has discrepancies to the given utility model.

Table 8: Mann-Whitney-U test for duration of static and dynamic preference adjustment

	Duration
N	62 participants
U	166
z	4.41
Asymptotic Sig. (2-sided test)	.000***
r	.56
***$p < 0.001$	

5.5.6 User Perception

To ensure the users' acceptance, we evaluate the dynamic adjustment process by the participants' subjective assessment in addition to the objective assessment. In addition to the objective duration and accuracy, we evaluate the participants' perceived duration and perceived accuracy. Moreover, as intrinsic motivation factors such as perceived enjoyment are relevant for predicting use intentions of utilitarian systems (Gerow et al. 2013), the user acceptance is assessed in terms of fun.

The perceived accuracy is a construct to measure the subjective quality of the solution. It measures the confidence of users of having achieved the best

Table 9:   Average arithmetic mean of constructs

	Perceived duration absolute	Perceived duration relative	Perceived accuracy	Fun
Scale	From 'very fast' to 'very slow' (7-point, inverted)	From 'much faster' to 'much slower' (7-point, inverted)	From 'very inaccurate' to 'very accurate' (7-point)	From 'do not agree at all' to 'strongly agree' (7-point)
M AVG static preference adjustment	2.59	2.50	6.02	3.98
M AVG dynamic preference adjustment	1.98	2.00	5.79	4.03

utility model. We measured it by five questions on a 7-point-Likert scale (adapted from Aloysius et al. 2006) in the survey shortly after the preference adjustment. In addition, the participants were asked for their perception of the duration of the preference adjustment. We used four questions for the perceived time needed (adapted from Dabholkar 1994) with two questions being formulated in an absolute manner ("took a long time", "was slow") and two questions being formulated in relation to the prior preference elicitation to rely on a reference point, which indicates the participant's individual speed. Therefore, we used the preference elicitation as reference, since all participants passed the same process independent of their treatment group ("less or more time compared to the preference elicitation", "slower or faster compared to preference elicitation"). Regarding fun, we used three empirically proven questions adapted from Dabholkar (1994). The questions applied can be found in appendix A3.

The scale of the perception of duration absolute and relative is inverted in the following section for better reading, indicating '1' very fast and '7' very slow. The average of the questions per construct ranges from 1.00 (M = 2.26, SD = 1.17) for the duration perception absolute and from 4.50 (M = 2.23, SD = 1.00) for the duration perception relative to 6.00 (both). The participants perceived the accuracy of their preferences in average very high (M = 5.90, SD = 0.97) with a broad range from 3.20 to 7.00 (on a scale from '1' very inaccurate to '7' very accurate). For fun, the full scale from 1.00 to 7.00 was used (M = 4.01, SD = 1.55). Table 9 shows the differences in the mean of the average per construct and per treatment group.

A principal component analysis (PCA) was conducted on the 16 items with orthogonal rotation (varimax). The Kaiser-Meyer-Olkin (KMO) measure verified the sampling adequacy for the analysis, KMO = .688. Bartlett's test of sphericity χ^2 (120) = 775.60, p < .001, indicated that correlations between items were sufficiently large for PCA. An initial analysis was run to obtain eigenvalues for each component in the data. Five components had eigenvalues over Kaiser's criterion of 1 and in combination explained 82.59% of the variance. Appendix A3 shows the factor loadings after rotation. The items that cluster on the same components suggest that component 1 represents perceived accuracy of preferences, component 2 negotiation experience, component 3 fun, component 4 absolutely perceived duration, and component 5 relatively perceived duration.

To evaluate discriminant validity, cross loadings between the factors are assessed. Appendix A3 shows a cross loading above the 0.2 level for the second question of relative perceived duration, which indicates that further analysis regarding relative perceived duration has to be performed with caution. However, each question loads higher on the associated construct than on any other construct, which assures good evidence of discriminant validity.

Regarding internal consistency reliability, Cronbach's α and composite reliability show values well above the thresholds of 0.7 (Nunnally and Bernstein 1994) except for relative perceived duration, which corresponds to the depicted cross loading of one of its items, see appendix A4. All factors matched the indicator reliability requirement of factor loadings over 0.4. Convergent validity of the constructs is analysed by its average variance extracted (AVE). AVE is greater than 0.5 for each construct, which means that the constructs explain more than half of the variance of their indicators, which is assumed to be sufficient.

Participants with dynamic preference adjustment perceive the time needed for the preference adjustment shorter than participants with static preference adjustment. For the perceived duration asked, the Mann-Whitney-U test does not show significant differences, although the duration of static adjustment is perceived longer (M = 2.59, SD = 1.34 from 1 "very short", "very fast" to 7 "very long", "very slow") than for dynamic adjustment (M = 1.98, SD = .93), U = 569, z = 1.28, ns, r = .16. However, a Mann-Whitney-U test of the perceived duration relatively asked shows a weak significant difference in the perceived time across the two preference adjustment processes, U = 622, z = 2.02, p < .05, r = .26, cf. Table 10. Dynamic preference adjustment is relatively perceived shorter (Mdn = 0.09) than static preference adjustment (Mdn = -0.17), showing a medium effect.

A Mann-Whitney U test shows no significant difference in the perceived accuracy across both preference adjustment methods (Mdn static adjustment = 0.52; Mdn dynamic adjustment = 0.17), U = 384, z = -1.33, ns, r = -.17. A Mann-Whitney U test shows for fun that there is no significant difference in fun across

Table 10: Mann-Whitney-U tests for static and dynamic preference adjustment

	Perceived duration absolute	Perceived duration relative	Perceived accuracy	Fun
N	62	62	62	62
U	569	622	384	477
z	1.28	2.02	1.33	0.02
Asymptotic Sig. (2-sided test)	.202	.043*	.182	.983
r	.16	.26	.17	.00
*p<0.05, **p<0.01, ***p<0.001				

the two preference adjustment methods (Mdn static adjustment = -0.08; Mdn dynamic adjustment = -0.00), U = 477, z = -0.02, ns, r = -.00, cf. Table 10.

5.6   Discussion

As mentioned in section 5.5.3, validation of multi-criteria decision analysis methods is difficult. A latitude of measures exists. As our aim is to design an efficient dynamic preference adjustment method, our major goal was to validate the efficiency of DynASE, i.e. its duration as other evaluation papers (cf. Meißner et al. 2011; Netzer and Srinivasan 2011; Schlereth et al. 2014). Objectively, our aim was achieved, since DynASE required significantly less time than a comparable static version (cf. section 5.5.5). In addition to the duration, DynASE required less questions than the static variant, and thus less effort independent of the individual duration. Both methods terminated when all issues were compared at least once. Whilst the static variant required eleven pairwise comparisons, for DynASE two were sufficient.

We showed that DynASE is applicable for dynamic preference measurement during electronic negotiations. All of the participants who were able to elicit their preferences in the first step (83.8 %) managed to adjust their preferences to get the given utility model, which shows the feasibility of DynASE.

We designed the evaluation using specified preferences as common in negotiation research (e.g. using the Inspire database as Kersten et al. 2017; Roszkowska and Wachowicz 2015b) to measure DynASE's convergent, discrimant, and predictive validity. However, as participants adjusted their preferences correctly, DynASE is not comparable to the static alternative in these measures.

Moreover, we surveyed the participants' perceptions of DynASE (since they play an important role in the method's reuse (Danielson and Ekenberg 2016)) and whether they value their decisions (Curhan et al. 2004). Perceived accuracy and fun were well above 'neutral', perceived duration was significantly shorter than the static alternative, although this construct has to be treated with caution, since one of the questions referring to the relative duration had a crossloading on the component of absolute duration.

The overall DynASE design has the advantage that rough importance weightings can be retrieved very quickly, since interpolation of the weightings is possible as soon as a ranking of the issues and three initial paired comparisons are conducted. This characteristic stems from the underlying ASE. This means that in changes resulting from additional issues or deletion of issues (cases A and F), preferences can already be adjusted using interpolation only if the ranking is adjusted. Comparisons are not even required to get rough importance weightings.

Mutli-criteria decision aiding can be grouped into four modern streams: 1) Value-focused approaches; 2) disaggregation methods; 3) multiobjective optimisation; and 4) outranking methods (Jacquet-Lagrèze and Siskos 2001). Multi-objective optimisation and outranking methods are not suitable for decision support in negotiations, since for decision support all possible alternatives must be assessable. While we chose a value-focused approach to be expanded by dynamic means, a method following the disaggregation-aggregation paradigm, such as robust ordinal regression methods, would also be conceivable. Robust ordinal regression (Greco et al. 2008) takes all compatible utility functions into account, that have been found instead of using only one. Inconsistencies of pairwise comparisons can be detected and resolved. Although robust ordinal regression methods can be used to determine a linear-additive utility model, it is required to select a representative utility function (Kadziński et al. 2012) to meaningfully be applicable for decision support (Spliet and Tervonen 2014).

As DynASE builds on ASE, it adopts its shortages. Multi-attribute utility theory has the restriction of independent issues and values. Hence, if real decision problems involve interdependencies between attributes, additive models do not fit (Spliet and Tervonen 2014). This led to different approaches, e.g. multiplicative and multi-linear value functions (Elsler and Schoop 2012; Jacquet-Lagrèze and Siskos 2001; Spliet and Tervonen 2014). Spliet and Tervonen (2014) propose that usually a set of additive value functions exists, which cover the preference information and also fulfil the assumption of mutual preferential independence. However, yet using an additive model, the participants could be asked directly for interdependencies or they could be asked in pairwise comparisons (Greco et al. 2014). Greco et al. (2014) propose a robust ordinal regression method with interacting criteria using an additive value preference model.

The assumptions made in chapter 5.2.1 imply some limitations of the method. The resulting utility function can only be an approximation to reality (cf. Luce and Raiffa 1957). Measured preferences "almost never satisfy the axioms" (Luce and Raiffa 1957, p. 35). Nevertheless, if true preferences can be elicited at all, DynASE provides an indicator for preference consistency. Same as in ASE, the applied log-linear multiple regression gives its coefficient of determination, which can give an indication of the preferential consistency.

Our empirical study is subject to the following limitations. Although DynASE is designed to efficiently adjust preferences in the required use cases, we only evaluated it by the use case (A) of a new issue. We cannot ensure its efficiency and subjective perception in the remaining use cases empirically. As laboratory experiment, it suffers from external validity as it is not investigated in a real negotiation setting. Moreover, the participants cover students, not practitioners. To lessen this limitation, we concentrated on graduate students trained in negotiation (Herbst and Schwarz 2011). However, this limitation remains. Nonetheless, our focus is on high internal validity. A quantitative approach in a real setting is not possible due to the incomparability of the negotiators' preferences.

5.7   Conclusion and Outlook

The aim of this paper is to design interactive dynamic preference measurement for an individual negotiator. The designed method is both objectively and subjectively more efficient than a static alternative. Thus, the main aim of the dynamic preference adjustment, improving the efficiency, is achieved. In our empirical study, DynASE required only half of the time of the static alternative for a single change. Moreover, the minimum time needed using DynASE was only 27.8 % of the minimum time needed using the static alternative. In application domains, where changes are welcomed, e.g. agile software development (Beck et al. 2001b), where thus all change scenarios occur multiple times, the method developed provides enormous values. In such a context, its efficiency facilitates to adjust one's preferences at all.

The contribution of this paper comprises of the designed method itself, the evaluation of DynASE proving the method's efficiency as well as its validity, and an additional perspective on the users' perception. Dynamic decision making problems with multiple, conflicting objectives appear in many real-world scenarios (Helbig et al. 2016; Nebro et al. 2018). However, research on expressing preferences is still scarce. The designed method is generalisable for application in specific domains, in which i) a large number of issues must be negotiated, ii) the agenda and/or preferences change during the negotiation, iii) decision support must be provided for an individual negotiator, for example such as requirements negotiations (cf. Lenz 2019; Reiser et al. 2012).

As shown in chapter 5.4, DynASE can easily be implemented in any negotiation support system or decision support system, which takes a linear-additive utility model as input to support decisions. Apart from the designed method itself, key elements for an efficient preference adjustment were found to be the separation of preferences and utility and the separate elicitation of preferences.

DynASE enables negotiation analysis (Raiffa et al. 2002) based on up-to-date preferences. The negotiation analysis serves the following purposes: comparison of own offers / offer drafts with the negotiation partner's offers and historical analysis of offers, own concessions and the negotiation partner's concessions.

Dynamic preference measurement provides a more accurate basis for decision making that enhances the effectiveness and efficiency of the negotiation process or the outcome of the process. An increase in effectiveness is realised by incorporating new or changing information during the process. Based on this, a continuous preference measurement respectively adjustment takes place. For example, it is expected that unnecessary messaging due to outdated preferences can be avoided. If preference adjustment will be used more often as it requires less effort so that preferences are consistently up-to-date remains to be seen.

Our empirical evaluation uses the case of a new issue with specified preferences. An empirical study without specified preferences, actively checking the consistency, combining different use cases, or application to other domains would be interesting for further confirmation. Furthermore, future research could address visualising or assessing previous offers dealing with outdated preferences.

6 Designing Dynamic Decision Support for Electronic Requirements Negotiations[4]

6.1 Introduction

To keep an overview of the various requirements in large software development projects is a great challenge, even if requirements management systems are employed. It gets even more challenging, if negotiations must be conducted, to determine, which requirements are actually implemented and how. Requirements negotiation is an "iterative process of communication and decision making between [stakeholders] who have the overall goal of agreeing on a software development process and outcome" (Lenz et al. 2015, p. 304). In such coordination and reconciliation processes, requirements to be implemented, their development cost, and the delivery schedule are negotiated (Grünbacher and Seyff 2005).

Decision support in such scenarios enables the quantification of requirements and possible alternatives of their implementations and thus makes them comparable (Vetschera 2006). In negotiations, in which various stakeholders (e.g. customers, developers, project managers, product owners) have a say, knowing one's own position and expressing this position quantitatively provides enormous benefits to enforce one's own interests.

A drawback is that software development is an industry characterised by a high degree of dynamics (Jarke and Lyytinen 2015). Especially in large software development projects, new information regarding requirements is obtained or disclosed throughout the project, so changes in requirements are likely (Hull et al. 2011). An existing set of requirements must be refined in subsequent iterations of the requirements negotiation process in terms of additional requirements, omitted requirements, and/or changes in existing requirements' scope (Boehm and Kitapci 2006; Grünbacher and Seyff 2005), which illustrates the high degree of uncertainty and incompleteness of information (Ngo-The and Ruhe 2005).

Moreover, negotiations underlie process dynamics which influence the negotiators' preferences (Curhan et al. 2004; Vetschera 2007). In general, prefer-

---

4   The content of this chapter is already published as: Annika Lenz, 2019, Designing Dynamic Decision Support for Electronic Requirements Negotiations. In: Thomas Ludwig, Volkmar Pipek (eds.) 14th International Conference on Wirtschaftsinformatik. Tagungsband. WI 2019. Universität Siegen, Germany, pp. 1160–1174, available at https://aisel.aisnet.org/wi2019/track10/papers/5/

© The Editor(s) (if applicable) and The Author(s), under exclusive license to Springer Fachmedien Wiesbaden GmbH, part of Springer Nature 2020
A. Lenz, *Dynamic Decision Support for Electronic Requirements Negotiations*, https://doi.org/10.1007/978-3-658-31175-9_6

ences are unstable due to new preference formation, learning or fatigue (Netzer et al. 2008). This effect is amplified by the negotiation partners' exchange during the negotiation process. By the negotiation partners' reciprocal behaviour they gain new information or achieve clarity about the negotiation issues or values, which influences their preferences (Reiser et al. 2012).

Thus, preference changes in requirements negotiations may stem from agenda changes (Fernandes 2016) or from the reciprocity of the negotiation process itself. In both cases, existing measurement of preferences must be efficiently adjusted to provide meaningful decision support. Dynamic decision support takes the perspective of time into consideration. It considers an unstable negotiation agenda (i.e. requirements or their implementation solution changes), and unstable preferences themselves.

From a requirements engineering perspective, decision making in requirements negotiations is supported by multi-criteria decision analysis approaches (e.g. Ruhe et al. 2002), which methodologically consider a dynamic perspective in their requirements negotiation process, however, do not carry it to the decision support process. Negotiation research delivers decision support dealing with incomplete information (e.g. Reiser 2013). However, literature, which integrates insights of both domains is still scarce (Grünbacher and Seyff 2005; Lenz et al. 2016). There is no comprehensive approach that focuses on supporting decisions in requirements negotiations on a dynamic, interactive level to allow for adjustment of preferences (cf. Lenz et al. 2016), although the necessity of dynamic methodologies for requirements negotiations is present (e.g. Boehm and Kitapci 2006; Reiser et al. 2012).

Against this background, our aim is to design efficient dynamic decision support in requirement negotiations integrating a requirements engineering and negotiation research perspective. Dynamic decision support enables continuously accurate preferences, which allows an accurate negotiation analysis (Raiffa et al. 2002), i.e. analysis of own and the negotiation partner's requirements specification offers and concessions. To this end, the aim of our paper is two-fold: (1) To design a dynamic decision support component for requirements negotiations; (2) to evaluate its suitability by comparing it with state-of-the-art decision support in electronic requirements negotiations using a scenario-based approach (Carroll 2000; Pohl 2010).

6.2 State-of-the-Art

In negotiations, the two perspectives of individual decision making and plural decision making are relevant (Raiffa et al. 2002). Decision analysis takes an individual perspective and focuses on a normative and prescriptive approach for an individual negotiator or a single negotiation party, while negotiation theory as a perspective of plural decision making assumes joint decision making. Negotiation theory describes how real people could make better collaborative decisions. Both perspectives are integrated in asymmetric negotiation analysis, which supports a negotiator's position considering the partner's behaviour (Reiser 2013) to support achieving the best outcome (Raiffa et al. 2002). Thus, decision support takes an individual decision making perspective in a joint decision making context, whose result and benefit is asymmetric negotiation analysis.

Prerequisite is that the individual preferences of the negotiating parties are measured before-hand. A multitude of preference measurement methods exists to quantify the decision makers' preferences. As terminology differs in the field of preference measurement methods, we refer to measuring preferences for attributes and alternatives. In self-explicated approaches (Eckert and Schaaf 2009), the decision makers elicit their preferences directly. The preference measurement can thus be carried out quickly and easily and the cognitive complexity can be kept low for the decision maker. For example, Adaptive Self-Explication (ASE, Netzer and Srinivasan 2011) comprises of three different user dialogue steps: (1) the alternatives are rated on a scale from 0 to 1; (2) the attributes are ranked regarding their importance; (3) pairwise comparisons of attributes are conducted, for which two attributes are presented to the decision maker, who enters a ratio of how much more important one attribute is compared to the other. Another popular preference measurement method is TOPSIS (Hwang et al. 1993), which uses linguistic terms to determine the attribute weightings.

Electronic negotiation systems aim to support the three phases of a negotiation, namely the planning phase (or pre-negotiation or preparation), the actual negotiation phase, and the post-settlement phase. Negotiation support systems have an inherent characteristic of providing decision support (Arnott and Pervan 2014). They help decision makers to understand the problem and assess the implications of their decisions. To do so, preference measurement methods are applied to calculate the utility of single offers using multi-attribute utility theory (Keeney and Raiffa 1976) based on the importance weightings of negotiation issues (= attributes) and issue values (= alternatives) (e.g. Kersten and Noronha 1999b; Schoop et al. 2003; Thiessen and Soberg 2003). The resulting utility model forms the basis for negotiation analysis (Raiffa et al. 2002).

Requirements engineering distinguishes between requirements and their implementation solutions (Pohl 2010). Using the terminology of preference measurement, requirements refer to attributes and solutions refer to alternatives. In requirements negotiations, three types of issues are negotiated: i) design related issues, ii) contract related issues, iii) technological issues and for each implementation solutions respectively options to resolve the issue (Grünbacher and

Seyff 2005; Herzwurm et al. 2012; Lenz and Schoop 2017 see chapter 3). For the sake of better reading, we refer to all types as requirements and their solutions.

Involved negotiation parties cover success critical stakeholders of the software development project (Boehm and Kitapci 2006), who typically pursue mismatching goals: Future end users desire numerous features, a high service level, or fast delivery, buyers may also wish timely delivery, however are also interested in cost within budget, or compliance, while developers prefer stable requirements and flexible contracts (Grünbacher and Seyff 2005). Typically, only a relevant subset of these stakeholders are actually involved in the respective negotiation, which results in different negotiation constellations (Fricker and Grünbacher 2008). Although requirements negotiation is an iterative process (Grünbacher and Seyff 2005), which is not a one-time episode but an on-going process in general, its instantiation characteristics depend on several factors such as the software development method deployed (e.g. traditional, agile, or hybrid software development), the project type, the collaboration situation (Grünbacher and Seyff 2005), involved stakeholders (Fricker and Grünbacher 2008), the project stage (beginning or completion of the project), negotiation scope (i.e. requirements and solutions, technologies, or contract aspects), or frequency. Thus, their structure may differ. Requirements negotiations can be performed in independent phases, each including respective stakeholders and resulting in a (partial) agreement (Fricker and Grünbacher 2008).

Nonetheless, in almost every software development project, requirements negotiations are present in some way, and in each requirements negotiation, decisions must be made. Decision support accordingly is required for stakeholders' conflicting requirements perspectives in the actual negotiation phase. We consider negotiations, in which preference measurement is supported electronically and analysis is provided based thereon. Preference measurement can jointly be conducted in face-to-face negotiation workshops (e.g. Boehm and Kitapci 2006) or be applied asynchronously for an individual decision maker to prepare the requirements negotiation (e.g. Schoop 2010).

The most widely used methodology in the area of interactive requirements negotiation support is the WinWin methodology (Boehm and Kitapci 2006; Lenz et al. 2016), which aims to achieve a fair agreement among all involved stakeholders by attempting to meet the win conditions of each stakeholder (Boehm and Kitapci 2006). Dealing with various stakeholders, group recommendation technologies, such as IntelliReq (Felfernig et al. 2012), dedicatedly aim to support collaboration and enable group decision making (Lenz et al. 2016). Based on the stakeholders' preferences, recommendation technologies are applied to reach a joint decision on which requirements to implement (first).

The presented existing approaches follow a dynamic paradigm and provide decision support, however dedicated preference adjustment mechanisms are missing. Applying dynamic preference measurement to the domain of requirements negotiations can improve such approaches substantially. Our work addresses the depicted gap by designing and evaluating such a concept.

6.3   Methodology

The methodology applied in this paper covers the design of dynamic decision support for requirements negotiations, DynaDeS, and the evaluation of the designed component, both based on scenarios to be captured (Arnott and Pervan 2014; Carroll 2000; Pohl 2010).

We design the component to fulfil the goal of providing dynamic decision support to handle preference changes efficiently. To do so, scenarios are considered, for which the design goal must be fulfilled (Carroll 2000; Pohl 2010). The scenarios affecting preference information changes, which must be supported, stem from volatile requirements (Grünbacher and Seyff 2005) and negotiation process dynamics (Curhan et al. 2004; Reiser et al. 2012), see Table 11. When requirements or solutions change during the negotiation process, the decision support component is intended to provide a process to adjust their preferences accordingly. Thus, it must consider (A) a new requirement with new solutions, (B) a new solution without a new requirement and adjust their preferences. Moreover, preferences are unstable and may change over time despite of requirements or solution changes, thus the decision support component must handle (C) preference changes for requirements and (D) preference changes for solutions.

To reach the overall aim of handling preference changes efficiently, the design process conducts the following steps: (1) Existing decision support of negotiation research is adapted to requirements negotiations; (2) the preference measurement is extended to allow dynamic preference adjustment; (3) the decision support processes are adapted to meaningfully use the adjusted preferences.

Table 11:   Scope of preference adjustment for dynamic decision support in requirements negotiations

#	Scenario	Cause
A	New requirement	Unstable requirements
B	New solution	Unstable requirements
C	Changed requirement preference	Negotiation process dynamics
D	Changed solution preference	Negotiation process dynamics

The designed DynaDeS is implemented in the web-based negotiation support system Negoisst (Schoop et al. 2003; Schoop 2010) to exploit the benefits of an integrated system. DynaDeS is evaluated by means of a scenario-based (Arnott and Pervan 2012; Pohl 2010) comparison to analyse whether the designed dynamic decision support component meets its design goals for requirements negotiations. Scenarios illustrate how design goals are satisfied (Pohl 2010). Thus, we compare DynaDeS to existing decision support w.r.t. their suitability for the required scenarios (cf. Table 11). Furthermore, as the WinWin methodology is the methodology most commonly used for electronic requirements negotiations (Lenz et al. 2016), we include decision support within the WinWin methodology (Boehm and Kitapci 2006; Kukreja and Boehm 2013). Moreover, we compare IntelliReq (Felfernig et al. 2012), which provides dedicated group decision support in requirements negotiations. Although the support components to compare are heterogeneous in different characteristics, they coincide in taking a dynamic perspective on decision support for requirements negotiations.

6.4   Design of the Dynamic Decision Support Component

The decision support component is not intended to replace requirements elicitation processes or requirements refinement processes. It starts when an initial set of requirements and their implementation solutions is determined. This set may be rudimentary at the beginning and be refined during the superordinate negotiation process, however, requirements and solution refinement is not meant to be part of the decision support component. In contrast, the decision support component is supposed to handle the required scenarios of changes of the environment.

6.4.1   A Concept for Dynamic Decision Support

In the following, we will (1) adapt existing decision support of negotiation research to requirements negotiations; (2) enable dynamic preference adjustment; (3) design processes to meaningfully use the adjusted preferences.

(1) For decision support during requirements negotiations without a dynamic perspective, in-formation about the agenda (i.e. requirements and solutions to negotiate) is gathered in the planning phase. The problem definition takes place based on the project goals and the project phase (cf. Grünbacher et al. 2006). At a very early stage, requirements negotiation involves negotiation issues on a high-level, while negotiation in a later stage of the software development project focuses on specific aspects or sub-projects. Requirements that are elicited at an early stage allow for a wide range of implementation solutions that will be specified later. Furthermore, in the planning phase success critical stakeholders' indi-

vidual goals are collected. These goals may concern high-level issues, general system functions, budget, schedule, or technical issues, such as the development environment. Having extracted the initial agenda to negotiate, the negotiation issues and values are elicited. Subsequently, still during the planning phase, an initial preference elicitation is performed, resulting in a (tentative) utility model, which is required to provide asymmetric analysis in the actual negotiation phase.

During the actual negotiation phase, the agreement takes place. The stakeholders exchange offers and counteroffers to find a mutually beneficial and acceptable solution. Analytical support is provided to assess own offers or offer drafts as well as the negotiation partner's offers based on the preferences measured.

(2) To provide dynamic preference adjustment, we choose ASE (Netzer and Srinivasan 2011) as basis preference measurement method, since it performs very well regarding its efficiency, validity, and cognitive complexity (Lenz and Schoop 2019 see chapter 4). Furthermore, although it is a one-shot preference measurement method as is common in multi-criteria decision analysis, it provides the potential to be adopted for dynamic contexts (Lenz and Schoop 2019 see chapter 4), since it uses scarcely dependencies between preference information and allows to separate preference information measured and a utility model calculated based thereon. In this paper, we incorporate DynASE, which extends ASE by dynamic preference mechanisms, into DynaDeS.

For the dynamic preference adjustment, similar user dialogues as in the initial preference elicitation are applied, namely rating of the desirability of all solutions, ranking of the requirements according to their importance, and pairwise comparison of all requirements (Netzer and Srinivasan 2011). After a bundle of pairwise comparisons is conducted, a utility model can be calculated. An adaptive selection of pairwise comparisons facilitates to ask for the greatest possible information gain. If the resulting utility model is sufficiently precise, the preference adjustment process terminates. Otherwise, further pairwise comparisons are conducted until a pre-defined number of comparisons is reached, or all issues are compared at least once.

(3) The decision support process is adapted to react to negotiation process dynamics and to embed subsequent activities in the actual negotiation phase. It allows to adjust preferences and to re-calculate the utility model during the actual negotiation phase and shifts thereby activities of the planning phase into the negotiation phase (similar to agenda negotiations, cf. Fernandes 2016), see Figure 13. Focus of the dynamic preference adjustment is the interaction of preference measurement and the utility model calculation. Most preference measurement methods do not separate the pure measurement of preferences from the calculation of the utility model. However, to enable efficient dynamic decision

Figure 13:   Dynamic decision support in the negotiation phases

support, the possibility of separation is inevitable. The preferences resulting from the initial preference elicitation must be saved independently of the utility model calculated to reuse still valid preferences in the case of changes.

In DynaDeS, the dynamic aspect comes into effect if new information is obtained, which result in (A) requirements, (B) solutions, (C) requirement preference, and/or (D) solution preference changes, see Figure 14. The planning phase is entered again in all scenarios. In the scenarios of A and B, additionally the agenda is adjusted. Subsequently in all scenarios, preferences are adjusted as well, dependent on the information gained: Solution ratings are maintained from the existing preference information if it is still valid. This can be facilitated because the solution ratings of one requirement do not relate to the ratings of other solutions. Except for scenario C when only requirement preference information changes, the first step of the preference measurement is repeated for (A) solutions of the new requirement, (B) a new solution, or (D) the outdated solution preference information. In the scenarios B and D where no requirement information has changed, the user dialogue is already completed and a renewed accurate utility model is calculated based on existing valid preference information and newly gathered preference information, which can be used in the stakeholder's analysis. For the scenarios of A and C, the preference adjustment process continues, presenting the existing requirements ranking to the user, in which (A) the new requirement must be sorted respectively (C) the rank of the respective requirement must be corrected. Preference information of paired comparisons of all other requirements is reused. Thus, based on the ranking and valid paired comparisons, a renewed utility model is calculated again. If the utility model is not yet sufficiently precise, additional pairwise comparisons involving the respective requirement can be performed. Optionally, an interactive check allows the stakeholders to view and validate their utility model and initiate preference adjustment in case the utility model does not fit their preferences (anymore). Again, based on a newly calculated utility model, precise analytical support can be provided.

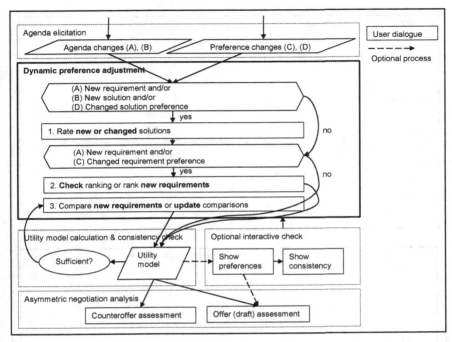

Figure 14:   DynaDeS

6.4.2   *Instantiation of Dynamic Decision Support in a Negotiation Support System*

The designed dynamic decision support is implemented in the negotiation sup-port system Negoisst (Schoop et al. 2003; Schoop 2010) as it already offers ho-listic negotiation support. Negoisst is a web-based support system, which pro-vides decision support, communication support, and document management. One aspect of its communication-orientation is to support the offer exchange by semi-structured message exchange, which allows to send unstructured text messages along with a structured, formal offer. To make binding offers, the negotiators send each other semi-structured messages in an alternating order.

Negoisst provides extensive analytical features for decision support (e.g. Reiser 2013). The analytical features enable to assess offers quantitatively based on the negotiators' preferences by utility values. The utility of offers can be ana-lysed by each negotiator. The history graph serves as visual support of the nego-tiators' convergence during the negotiation process, depicting the utility of offers

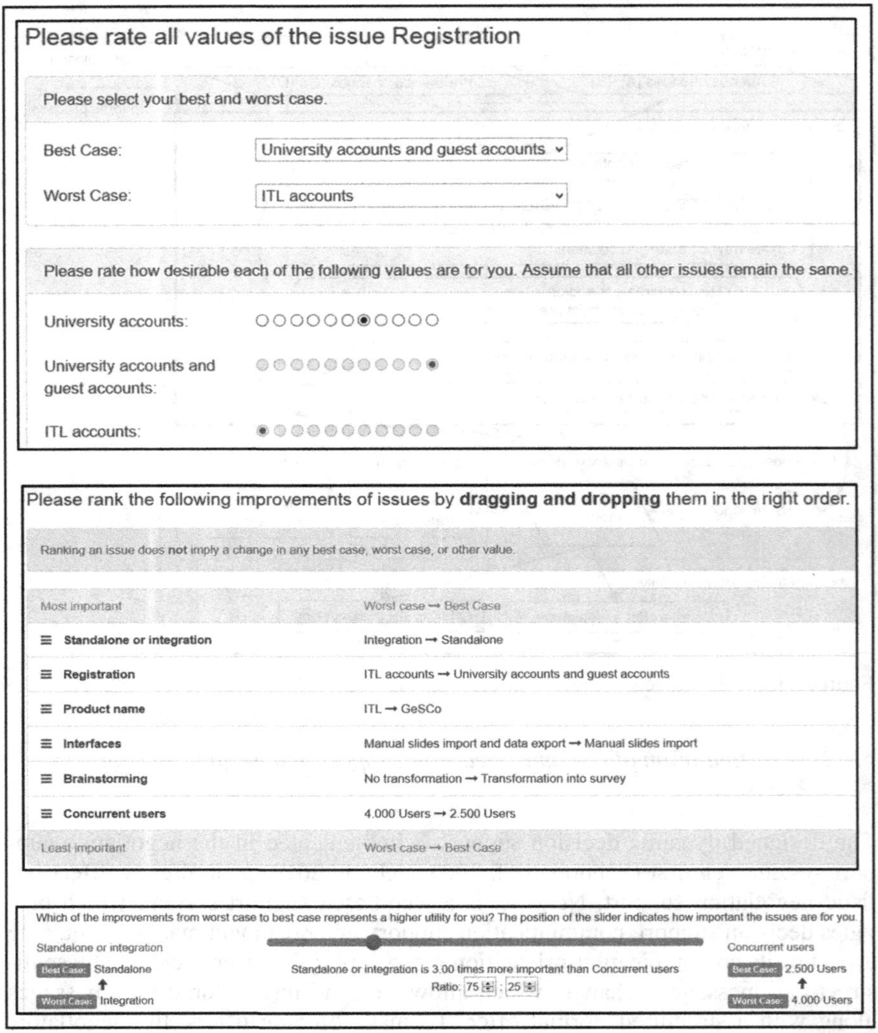

Figure 15:   Preference adjustment in Negoisst: Rating of solutions, ranking of requirements, and pairwise comparison of requirements

over time. Concessions and gains can be analysed visually. Negoisst provides analytical support during the phases of planning (e.g. preference elicitation) and in the phase of negotiation (e.g. offer assessment and analysis). The implementation of the preference adjustment within DynaDeS covers the following three user dialogues: (1) Rating of solutions; (2) ranking of requirements; (3) comparing requirements pairwise by using a slider or input fields, see Figure 15.

6.5 Scenario-Based Comparison of Dynamic Decision Support for Requirements Negotiation

In the following, we will analyse in a scenario-based (Arnott and Pervan 2012; Pohl 2010) comparison as to whether DynaDeS meets its design goals for requirements negotiations. DynaDeS will be compared with decision support based on the WinWin methodology (Kukreja and Boehm 2013) and IntelliReq (Felfernig et al. 2012).

6.5.1   Characteristics of the Decision Support Components

The three decision support components all quantify the assessment of requirements and/or solutions. However, they use different assessment bases to provide decision support. In a late incorporation of the WinWin methodology, subsequently called WinWin, TOPSIS is used, which assesses strategic business goals and requirements based on ease of realisation, their business value, and relative penalty (Kukreja and Boehm 2013), while IntelliReq requests the user to rate one of the solutions for a requirement as the preferred solution (Felfernig et al. 2012). Requirements are not assessed. In contrast, DynaDeS uses utility functions to assess requirements and their solutions. It assesses the requirements relatively dependent on all requirements, while the solutions are assessed independently determining one most preferred, one least preferred solution and rating all other solutions directly on a scale from 0 to 1 per requirement.

Regarding the actual support for the negotiators to make their decisions, WinWin focuses on making well-informed decisions based on cost, benefit, and penalty. It additionally considers the requirements' contribution to business goals and performs a relative assessment, so requirements and their solutions can be compared with each other. IntelliReq provides a recommendation for the group of stakeholders, which is based on the preferences of all group members. The stakeholders' assessments do not relate to each other, nor do the assessment of the requirements relate to each other. DynaDeS assesses solutions for requirements under consideration in terms of utility based on the solution preferences and the relative importance of a requirement to facilitate utility analysis (Bergsmann 2014; Raiffa et al. 2002).

The process for requirements negotiations using the WinWin methodology follows an iterative spiral model. Adjustments can be conducted in each iteration and decision support is correspondingly provided in each iteration when the win conditions are reconciled (Boehm and Kitapci 2006). IntelliReq is intended to be used in any existing requirements negotiation process model. Since it is not embedded in a process, stakeholders can change their preferences any time as long as the process has not completed resulting in a group recommendation. DynaDeS allows an iterative refinement throughout the negotiation process. Preference adjustments can be conducted at any time to provide updated accurate decision support when asymmetric analysis in the negotiation process is needed.

The concept of requirements and solutions is viewed differently in the three decision support components. The WinWin methodology elicits and negotiates win conditions, issues, and options. To consolidate terminology, we refer to issues as requirements and options as solutions. IntelliReq uses requirements and decision alternatives. Here, we refer to decision alternatives as solutions, too. DynaDeS emerges from general electronic negotiation support. Here, negotiation issues are referred to as requirements and issue values are referred to as solutions.

6.5.2   Comparison of the Decision Support Components

In the following (see Table 12), we analyse WinWin, IntelliReq, and DynaDeS based on the scenarios from Table 11. Following the WinWin extensions of the spiral model (Boehm and Kitapci 2006), for scenario A, in each iteration a new requirement can be added. The subsequent steps need to be performed, which are to generate solutions to cover the requirement and to jointly agree upon both the new requirement and its solutions. The new requirement has to be assigned to business goals to correctly assess its value. The preference measurement must be repeated. A new solution for a requirement (B) can also be added in each iteration. The solution possibly makes agreements obsolete, so in the same iteration, agreements possibly need to be dissolved and a new agreement must be made involving the new solution. Scenario B does not impact decision support, since solutions are not assessed. The process does not foresee that a stakeholder's preference may change after a requirement is assessed as required in scenario C. A repetition of the assessment and calculation is required. If a stakeholder's preference for a solution (D) has changed, is not applicable in WinWin, since solution preference information is not elicited and included in decision support.

In IntelliReq, adding a new requirement (A) is not designed. However, adding requirements to the agenda should be possible as long as the superordinate negotiation process is not concluded. For the new requirement solutions have to be entered and all stakeholders must utter their preferences for the best solution. The recommendation process must be repeated from scratch including the new

Table 12:   Comparison of decision support components for requirements negotiations

	Scenario A	Scenario B	Scenario C	Scenario D
WinWin (Kukreja and Boehm 2013)	Repeat preference measurement	No impact on decision support	Repeat assessment for the respec-tive requirement	Not applicable
IntelliReq (Felfernig et al. 2012)	Repeat recommendation process	Repeat recommendation process	Not applicable	Repeat recommendation process
DynaDeS	Rate solutions of new requirement; insert requirement into ranking; optionally conduct two requirement comparisons; repeat calculation of utility model	Rate new solution; repeat calculation of utility model	Check requirements ranking; conduct two requirement comparisons; repeat calculation of utility model	Assess solution; repeat calculation of utility model

requirement, so decision support can be provided. A new solution (B) is also not foreseen but should be possible to be added at any time. As in scenario A, all stakeholders must consider if the new solution is their most preferred solution and enter it accordingly. The recommendation process must be repeated again. Scenario C is not applicable since requirements are not assessed in IntelliReq. Thus, decision support regarding requirements is not provided. Stakeholders can add or change (D) preferences for solutions at any time. IntelliReq does not use a preference measurement method, but asks for the most preferred solution, while the remaining solutions are not assessed. Thus, changes can be made very easily and quickly. Subsequently the recommendation process must be repeated again.

In DynaDeS, in case of a new requirement (A), all solution preferences can be maintained. Only the solutions of the new requirement have to be assessed. The existing requirements ranking can be reused, too. The ranking is presented to the stakeholder who only must sort in the new requirement. All paired comparisons can be kept. At this point, a utility model can already be calculated, because the relative importance weight of the new requirement can be interpolated based on the requirements ranking. The usual criteria terminate the adjustment process, i.e. two comparisons including the new requirement can be performed if desired. If a new solution is added (B) to an existing requirement, which does not replace the best or worst solution of the respective requirement, it is rated as in scenario A. The partial utility value of the newly rated solution is included in the utility model. In case the preference information for a requirement changes (C), the requirements ranking must be checked respectively corrected and all related paired comparisons must be adjusted. Based thereon, the utility model can be re-calculated. If the preference information of an existing solution has changed (D), the preference adjustment process is the same as in scenario B. The respective requirement and its solution ratings is presented to the stakeholder, who corrects the respective assessment.

6.6   Discussion and Conclusions

The scenario-based evaluation shows that although both decision support components besides DynaDeS follow dynamic approaches, they do not support preference adjustment reusing the existing assessment. It is required to repeat preference measurement instead of only adjusting changes. Consequentially, the applied preference measurement methods require repeated information input. This is the major advantage of DynaDeS: The analysed decision support component based on the WinWin methodology cannot deal with changes efficiently. Using DynaDeS, the correction of the requirement ranking is already sufficient to measure the relative importance of an issue based on valid relative importance weightings of other requirements. If a more accurate importance weighting is desired, two pairwise comparisons are sufficient.

The main contributions of this paper are the dynamic concept and the proposed decision support process to integrate it. The adjustment of preferences during the requirements negotiation process provides a more accurate basis for decision making that improves the effectiveness and efficiency of the requirements negotiation process. An increase in effectiveness is reached by incorporating new or changing information during the process. Key concepts are both the separation of preferences and utility and relating preferences only to one other object. The general concept can be used and adopted by existing approaches for decision support in requirements negotiations to extend their work. The scenario-based evaluation shows the general applicability of a dynamic perspective as an improvement to decision support. Implications for practice relate to the facilitation of quickly adjusting single preferences, representing the stakeholders' interests, and thus relying on accurate decision support.

Future research could address integrating dependencies between requirements and assumptions of multi-attribute utility theory, since it requires attributes must be independent of each other. Another extension to this work could address an additional level of criteria. Stakeholders may use various criteria to assess requirements or their implementation solutions. For example, customers may evaluate requirements according to their importance, the budget, or the time of delivery, while developers use profitability and availability of resources. Dynamic decision support could enable individual criteria.

Moreover, research proposes that visualisation of information respectively the decision problem should both match the individual's cognitive style and the decision task characteristics (Engin and Vetschera 2017). The decision maker's experience could be considered as well (Gettinger and Koeszegi 2014). Future studies could investigate, which type of visualisation in requirements negotiation is the most appropriate one. Different types of visualisation and information input could be provided so that an individual decision maker can pick the most appropriate one, e.g. regarding the presentation of the pairwise comparisons in the preference adjustment process. Additionally to different input types, the ratio of the comparison could be provided in numbers, in bars or in a bar chart.

6.7   Acknowledgements

The author gratefully acknowledges her PhD scholarship from the State Baden-Württemberg and the support of the research area "Negotiation Research – Transformation, Technology, Media, and Costs", Faculty of Business, Economics, and Social Sciences at the University of Hohenheim.

7 Discussion and Outlook

The following chapter summarises, discusses, and evaluates the findings of this thesis with a critical acclaim. Its contribution is classified by the knowledge contribution framework in design science research (Gregor and Hevner 2013). This thesis concludes with an outlook for future research in the field of decision support for requirements negotiations.

7.1 Summary

The overarching objective of this thesis is to enable efficient dynamic decision support in electronic requirements negotiations. To reach this objective, this thesis designs, implements and evaluates a concept for dynamic decision support in requirements negotiations. The overall design goals are to handle preference changes efficiently and enable accurate measurement of preferences changed, which corresponds to the decision makers' perception.

In order to achieve this, the following two research questions are formulated. Research question 1 "Which factors determine the decision context in requirements negotiations?" aims at the general requirements for the concept of dynamic decision support in requirements negotiations and thus lays the foundations for the overall goal. It comprises of the four sub-goals to identify relevant decision problem structures, requirements for a dynamic preference measurement method, change scenarios in requirements negotiations, and issue types in requirements negotiations as depicted in Figure 16. Research question 2 "How can an individual negotiator be supported best in his or her decisions in requirements negotiations?" aims to design a concept by building upon this basis. It addresses the design in two artefacts: The design of a preference measurement method, which captures the decision problem and preference dynamics; and the design of a decision support component, which applies dynamic adjustments from dynamic preference measurement. The design of the dynamic preference measurement method is developed in two sub-goals: The assessment of static preference measurement methods; and the extension of the most suitable one to meet dynamic demands.

Chapter two provides theoretical background for decision support in electronic requirements negotiations by integrating a negotiation theoretic perspective and a requirements engineering perspective. Based thereon a research

A. Lenz, *Dynamic Decision Support for Electronic Requirements Negotiations*, https://doi.org/10.1007/978-3-658-31175-9_7

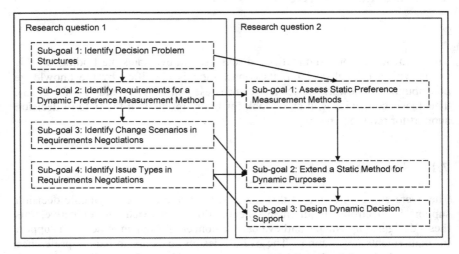

Figure 16:   Sub-goals of research questions 1 and 2 and their relations

process within the design science research framework (Hevner et al. 2004) is developed, which employs both perspectives by making use of solutions developed in negotiation research considering domain knowledge from requirements engineering research. From preference measurement in electronic negotiations as routine design, this thesis develops dynamic preference adjustment in electronic negotiations as an improvement and decision support in electronic requirements negotiations as exaptation leading to the design of dynamic decision support in electronic requirements negotiations as invention.

Chapters three to six address the research questions 1 and 2 as depicted in Figure 17. Chapter three addresses solely research question 1 by providing decision problem structure matrices. The first sub-goal of research question 1 concerns the decision problem structure in requirements negotiations. Considering both the traditional and the agile software development paradigm, two matrices of how the decision problem is possibly structured, are delivered (cf. chapter 3.3.3). As a result, focus is set on the most relevant decision problem structure, which consists of an objective, negotiation issues, and negotiation alternatives. Figure 18 highlights the decision problems from chapters 3.3.1 and 3.3.2, which follow the structure under consideration (green). In negotiations within the context of traditional requirements engineering, this structure can be applied to requirements as negotiation issues and solutions as negotiation alternatives as well as to packages as negotiation issues and solutions as their negotiation alternatives. In negotiations within the context of agile requirements engineering,

3 Decision Problems in Requirements Negotiations – Identifying the Underlying Structures

> **Research question 1, sub-goal 1:**
> Identify Decision Problem Structures
> chapter 3.3.3

4 Assessment of Multi-Criteria Preference Measurement Methods for a Dynamic Environment

> **Research question 1, sub-goal 2:**
> Identify Requirements for a Dynamic Preference Measurement Method
> chapter 4.3.1

> **Research question 2, sub-goal 1:**
> Assess Static Preference Measurement Methods
> chapter 4.4.3

5 DynASE – A Method for Dynamic Preference Adjustment in Electronic Negotiations

> **Research question 1, sub-goal 3:**
> Identify Change Scenarios in Requirements Negotiations
> chapter 5.3

> **Research question 1, sub-goal 4:**
> Identify Issue Types in Requirements Negotiations
> chapter 5.5.2

> **Research question 2, sub-goal 2:**
> Extend a Static Method for Dynamic Purposes
> chapter 5.3

6 Designing Dynamic Decision Support for Electronic Requirements Negotiations

> **Research question 2, sub-goal 3:**
> Design Dynamic Decision Support
> chapter 6.4.1

Figure 17:   Contributions of chapters 3 to 6 to research questions 1 and 2

requirements are structured as negotiation issues and either their prioritisation is modelled as negotiation alternative or the assignment to an iteration is modelled as negotiation alternative. Consequently, the subsequent chapters refer to this decision problem structure.

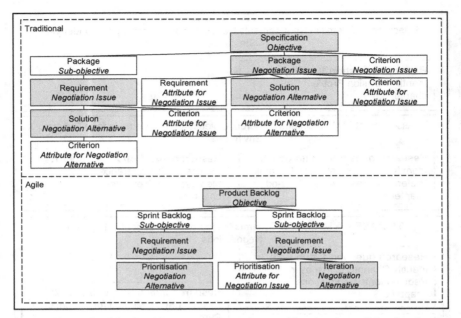

Figure 18:   Decision problem structures under consideration in traditional and agile requirements negotiations

Chapters four and five both deliver sub-goals of research question 1 and research question 2. Building on the decision problem structure to focus on, chapter four preselects preference measurement methods and assesses them towards their suitability for dynamic preference measurement. In order to achieve this, it identifies requirements for a dynamic preference measurement method for negotiations to fulfil the second sub-goal of research question 1, which are to facilitate individual preference measurement; allow changes in the scope of the decision problem, i.e. adding and withdrawing of attributes and alternatives; complement preferences for additional elements efficiently without distorting existing preferences; and adjust the measurement to preference changes efficiently.

Based on the decision problem structure and the requirements identified, chapter four assesses static preference measurement methods to address sub-goal 1 of research question 2. To conceptualise the design of a dynamic preference measurement method, the state-of-the-art preference measurement methods ASE (Netzer and Srinivasan 2011), PASE (Schlereth et al. 2014), PCPM (Scholz et al. 2010), ACA (Johnson 1987; Sawtooth Software, Inc. 2007), FastPACE (Toubia et al. 2003), and CARDS (Dahan et al. 2004) are assessed in chapter 4.4.3 referring to their suitability for dynamic scenarios and their potential to be expanded by both a qualitative and a quantitative assessment. The qualitative assessment covers the fulfilment of the requirements identified and their possibility to expand them to meet the requirements building upon research question 1, whilst the quantitative assessment assesses their performance. Three empirical studies are utilised to evaluate their efficiency, validity, and survey difficulty. The overall assessment shows that among the six preselected preference measurement methods, the ASE is the most suitable one. Although it is slightly less efficient than PCPM and slightly more difficult than PCPM, it shows higher potential to be expanded to meet dynamic demands. Consequently, the ASE is chosen to be extended as a dynamic preference measurement method.

Chapter five develops and evaluates the dynamic preference measurement method DynASE. In order to achieve this, it identifies change scenarios (cf. chapter 5.3) building upon the requirements identified in chapter 4. The fulfilment of requirement 1, enabling preference measurement for an individual decision maker, is already ensured by the selection of ASE, which is why it is considered as fulfilled and thus not part of the following change scenarios: The use case of measuring preferences of a new requirement with new solutions in relation to existing preferences of other requirements and their solutions; measuring preferences of a new solution for an existing requirement in relation to existing preferences of other solutions; adjusting preferences of a solution; adjusting preferences of a requirement; in case of deleting requirements or solutions, which impact/affect relative preferences of other requirements and/or solutions, adjusting their relative preference measurement. Moreover, it aims to identify types of issues, which are negotiated (sub-goal 4 of research question 1). Thereby, this thesis addresses, how this decision problem structure is designed with respect to different issues to be negotiated in requirements negotiations. Three types of negotiation issues are identified in this thesis: Issues related to design; issues related to the contract; and issues related to technology.

Building on chapter four, the most suitable static preference measurement method is extended for dynamic purposes. A design is proposed, which addresses efficient dynamic preference measurement utilising mechanisms of the ASE. The developed dynamic preference measurement method DynASE is implemented in the negotiation support system Negoisst (Schoop et al. 2003; Schoop 2010) to evaluate its fulfilment of the design goals empirically in a laboratory experiment using a requirements negotiation case study. As benchmark a static design alternative of the ASE is implemented as well, which requires the repetitive elicitation of preferences to be applied in a dynamic context at all. The requirements negotiation case study considers all three different types of negotiation issues identified: Two design related issues; three technology related issues; and two contract related issues (cf. chapter 5.5.2). The empirical study confirms the efficiency of the dynamic method developed: Participants using DynASE adjusted their preferences significantly faster than their control group using the static design alternative (cf. chapter 5.5.5), while both providing objectively accurate results (cf. chapter 5.5.4) and the participants perceiving these results as accurate (cf. chapter 5.5.6).

Chapter six on the contrary, concluding the studies solely answers a sub-goal of research question 2. It adapts the decision support component in electronic negotiations to design a concept for dynamic decision support, incorporates DynASE, addressing the decision problem structure identified and the change scenarios derived in research question 1 (cf. chapter 6.4.1). Chapter six evaluates the developed concept for dynamic decision support, DynaDeS, by a scenario-based comparison with two other decision support components for requirements negotiations, namely IntelliReq (Felfernig et al. 2012) and a component based on the WinWin methodology (Kukreja and Boehm 2013) on the basis of the change scenarios identified (cf. chapter 6.5.2). The evaluation demonstrates that DynaDeS is superior to the two components by reusing existing preferences in the case of changes of the decision problem or preferences of related requirements and/or solutions. In this way, DynaDeS manages to avoid repetition of preference elicitation tasks, which makes it efficient.

The results of this thesis show that the general dynamic decision support component is applicable for different scenarios of requirements negotiations. Major advantages of the designed dynamic decision support are its efficiency and its applicability to different change scenarios.

7.2   Discussion

In multi-criteria decision aiding, four modern streams have evolved (cf. chapter 5.6): 1) Value-focused approaches; 2) disaggregation methods; 3) multi-objective optimisation; and 4) outranking methods (Jacquet-Lagrèze and Siskos 2001). Due to the fact that multi-objective optimisation (stream 3) and outranking methods (stream 4) cannot be used for decision support in negotiations, as negotiation analysis requires the assessment of all possible alternatives, this thesis chooses a value-focused approach following multi-attribute utility theory (stream 1). Although applying linear-additive utility functions is state-of-the-art in decision support for negotiations, cf. state-of-the-art negotiation support systems such as Inspire (Kersten and Noronha 1999a), Negoisst (Schoop 2010), or SmartSettle (Thiessen and Soberg 2003), multi-attribute utility theory underlies the assumption of independent attributes and values. However, real-world decision problems may involve interdependencies between attributes, for which additive models do not fit (Spliet and Tervonen 2014). Thus, it is to discuss, if a linear partial utility function for numerical issues is appropriate. This led to different approaches, e.g. multiplicative and multilinear value functions (Elsler and Schoop 2012; Jacquet-Lagrèze and Siskos 2001; Spliet and Tervonen 2014). Another suggestion is that typically a set of additive functions exists, which cover the preference information and also fulfil the assumption of mutually independent preferences (Spliet and Tervonen 2014). While this thesis chooses a value-focused approach to decision making, a method following the disaggregation-aggregation paradigm (stream 2) is also conceivable. Robust ordinal regression (Greco et al. 2008) results in a set of compatible utility functions. It can be used too, to determine a linear-additive utility model. To meaningfully apply robust ordinal regression for decision support, a representative utility function must be selected (Kadziński et al. 2012; Spliet and Tervonen 2014).

The specialty of the designed dynamic decision support for requirements negotiations is the refinement of high-level issues later on, which may require activity, which is usually done in the pre-negotiation phase such as preference elicitation for negotiation issues and values. The designed process allows to shift activities from the preparation phase to the actual negotiation phase, and thus allows to use the process steps and functionality of the pre-negotiation phase during the actual negotiation phase (cf. chapter 6.4.1). Similar to the phase model including agenda negotiation, which provides the possibility to switch back and forth between the phases of agenda negotiation, preference elicitation, and value negotiation (cf. Fernandes 2016), the proposed process facilitates flexible switching of the phases. Figure 19 shows the components of agenda elicitation, preference elicitation, and utility model calculation used in the planning phase.

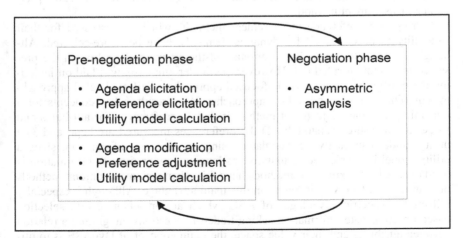

Figure 19: Activities of dynamic decision support during the negotiation process (based on chapter 6)

The designed process enables using adjustment functions of these components after the negotiation phase has already started, namely agenda changes, preference adjustment, and the re-calculation of the utility model. Although it is argued that the preparation phase is the most important phase in negotiations it is often not effectively performed in practice (Thompson 2012). The significance of the preparation does not diminish when a dynamic decision support process is used. On the contrary, additional planning is required in asynchronous phases during a negotiation.

7.3 Limitations

This thesis is subject to the following limitations, which need to be taken into consideration in order to adequately interpret the implications of the findings. A design science research approach was chosen to fulfil the research goal of this thesis, of which an inherent characteristic is to strongly interlock research and practice to ensure relevance of the phenomenon under investigation. As this thesis draws the fundamental status quo of the research area from literature, the results may be limited. To remedy this limitation, it was intended to build on literature, which builds upon empirical results and reflects empirical studies. Moreover, it is aimed to gain a comprehensive picture of the status quo by eliciting a broad context of decision support in requirements negotiations, namely the decision problem structure, change scenarios in requirements negotiations, types of issues in requirements negotiations, and thus requirements for a dynamic preference measurement method.

Promising preference measurement methods, which are assessed for their suitability to be expanded for dynamic demands, have been pre-selected. Although the pre-selection is based on state-of-the-art methods, a bias in the pre-selection cannot be ruled out. However, particular emphasis was laid on including three different types of value-focused approaches: Self-explicated approaches, conjoint analyses, and hybrid approaches. As a result, a key concepts for a dynamic preference adjustment method is that 1) preferences for attributes and values are measured separately; 2) the preferences measured are kept; and 3) a utility model can easily be calculated using the existing information, since a utility model is considered as tentative as long as new preference information is available. All self-explicated methods have this advantage over conjoint methods or hybrid ones. DynASE is based on this main advantage. Although it especially utilises the specific advantages of ASE, which are an adaptive task selection based on up-to-date information asking trade-off questions integrating a relation between attributes and their value space, the main concept of DynASE is to utilise the above described general advantages of self-explicated approaches.

Contrary to the design science research paradigm, the designed dynamic decision support component was not evaluated in a practical environment. Moreover, an empirical evaluation was conducted only for one case – the case of a new issue (see chapter 5.5). However, this was counteracted in two ways: The most complex scenario was chosen for empirical evaluation, which aims to ensure that less complex scenarios are supported efficiently too, and the remaining scenarios were descriptively evaluated based on hypothetic case study design. A comparison with other state-of-the-art approaches of the scenarios to address complements the evaluation.

Although laboratory experiments are an adequate approach to evaluate design science research (Hevner et al. 2004), they underlie a low external validity. A static design alternative was specifically developed to serve as a realistic benchmark in the laboratory experiment. The static design alternative was used to evaluate the intended improvement by the dynamic design alternative (Gregor and Jones 2007; Hevner and Chatterjee 2010). Moreover, pre-constructed preference models were applied instead of measuring the participants' 'real' preferences to ensure there will be one – and only one – preference change of the desired use case scenario. Allowing the participants to measure their actual preferences, the rigour of the experimental setting is challenged, since it is not predictable, which change scenarios happen or if they happen at all. If participants changed their preferences, they might have external intentions, e.g. adjusting their preferences last minute in alignment with an upcoming outcome to gain a better grade. Although external validity of the study is reduced by using pre-constructed preference models and enforcing one specific scenario change, which limit naturalistic behaviour, these two constraints are set intentionally to increase internal validity. Moreover, the participants cover students, not practitioners. To shorten this limitation, graduate students trained in negotiation participated in the study as the external validity of research based on trained student samples has been proven for negotiation research (Herbst and Schwarz 2011). However, this limitation remains. Nonetheless, the focus lies on high internal validity. The advantage of choosing a laboratory experiment is to enable assessment and comparisons of the participants' resulting preferences.

7.4   Contribution

This doctoral thesis delivers several level 1 and level 2 artefacts (cf. Gregor and Hevner 2013). Level 1 artefacts cover the instantiation of the static preference adjustment design alternative, the dynamic design alternative "DynASE", and the instantiation of the incorporating dynamic decision support process "DynaDeS".

Within the broad context of dynamic decision support in requirements negotiations, level 2 artefacts comprise of the conceptualisation of the static design
alternative and the dynamic design alternative as well as the dynamic decision
support component. Moreover, this thesis extracted key concepts for an efficient
dynamic preference adjustment method as design principles: Compositional
(self-explicated) preference measurement methods are better suited than decompositional or hybrid methods, since they measure preferences for attributes and
values separately, which makes them flexible to adjust preferences. Requiring
few preference relations is a key concept for efficient preference adjustment. The
more preference relations are required, the more complex is adjusting the measurement of single preferences. Relying on only few preference relations, however, threatens their overall validity. The ASE only uses preference relations between attributes, preference relations between values of one attribute, and
ensures cross relations by the range between an attribute's best and worst case
compared to the other attributes' ranges between their best and worst case. As a
result, ASE needs only few preference relations to extract valid preferences.
Moreover, for an efficient preference adjustment, separation of preferences and
the utility model is required to adjust single preferences flexibly.

In order to put the research contribution into perspective, the knowledge
contribution framework is used to classify the contribution according to its application domain maturity and its solution maturity (Gregor and Hevner 2013). The
mature solution of preference elicitation and decision support in electronic negotiations is extended to the immature application domain of decisions in requirements negotiations. Second, the solution of DynASE (dynamic preference adjustment, see chapter 5.3) is proposed, which belongs to the improvement-
quadrant. These two contributions have been utilised to develop the solution
DynaDeS (dynamic decision support, see chapter 6.4) in electronic requirements
negotiations, which represents an innovation. The general applicability of a dynamic perspective is an improvement to decision support, see Figure 20.
DynASE and DynaDeS can be used and adopted by existing approaches for
decision support in requirements negotiations to extend their work.

The proposed dynamic preference adjustment method and the designed dynamic decision support facilitate a requirements negotiation analysis based on
accurate preferences for the following analysis purposes: 1) Comparison of own
specification offers (or drafts) with the negotiating partner's offer, which is currently on the table; 2) analysis of the requirements to be implemented and identification of the most important requirements; 3) progression analysis of offers,
concessions, and gains; 4) comparison of the specification to be accepted with
the own aspiration level and reservation level.

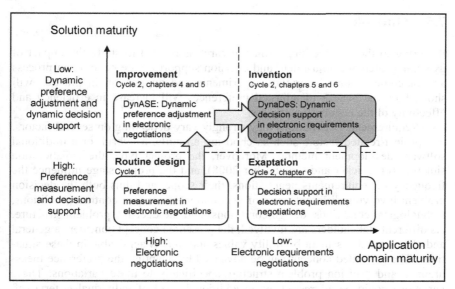

Figure 20: Classification of the artefacts by the knowledge contribution framework (adapted from Gregor and Hevner 2013, p. 345)

Dynamic preference measurement and corresponding decision support provide a more accurate basis for decision making that improves the effectiveness and efficiency of the requirements negotiation process. An increase in effectiveness is reached by incorporating new or changing information during the process. Using up-to-date information, continuous adjustment of the preference measurement is enabled. For example, it is expected that unnecessary exchange of the negotiation partners based on outdated preferences can be avoided. Efficiency is increased by relating the result to the most accurate possible preferences. A big advantage is that the criteria for preferences can be set individually by each negotiating party. For example, while the customers want to have based their decisions on business value, developers may refer to the complexity of the implementation, both measure their preferences in utility values.

7.5   Outlook

Referring to the last section, further research is needed to study the impact of dynamic preference adjustment and decision support on the negotiation process and outcome. Future laboratory experiments and application in practice will show, how the benefit of adjusted preferences will increase in efficiency and effectivity of the negotiation process.

Requirements negotiations may strongly vary depending on several factors, e.g. project-related factors such as choosing an agile, a hybrid, or a traditional software development method. Moreover, the project type, the collaboration situation (cf. Fricker and Grünbacher 2008), and the project stage influence the frequency of requirements negotiations, their scope, and thus both the decision problem involving different types of negotiation issues (i.e. contract conditions, technological conditions, design conditions) and the decision problem structure. As different stakeholders are involved, the presented concept considers a general and abstracted assessment by utility values and thus is applicable in these situations. The presented concept can be advanced by adapting the preference measurement and decision problem structure specifically to these variations. These variations could be addressed by an additional level of individual criteria (cf. chapter 3) to introduce a context-related measure to the utility values. For example, a developer could assess costs for requirements and solutions and relate these costs to a certain utility value.

Stakeholders may not only base their decisions on different criteria, they also take different roles, pursue different aims, and have different knowledge. Stakeholders may be experts in their own domain and lay people in the negotiation partner's domain. Thus, an individualisation of the dynamic decision support or its visualisation could consider the stakeholder's individual cognitive style and the decision task characteristics (cf. Engin and Vetschera 2017) as well as the stakeholder's experience in requirements negotiations (cf. Gettinger and Koeszegi 2014) in future work.

Introducing the dimension of time to preference-based decision support bring several aspects into focus. The process of concession making is not only important for the overall outcome of the negotiation (Vetschera 2016) but more importantly pivotal for the negotiation parties reaching an agreement or terminating the negotiation without a resolution (Vetschera and Filzmoser 2012). Central activities in the concession making phase of negotiations are to compare offers and counteroffers, from which behaviour patterns may be derived to predict the progression of the negotiation (Gettinger and Koeszegi 2014). To support concession making, negotiation support systems with analytic features often provide visualisation of the offer progression (cf. Gettinger et al. 2012; Gettinger and Koeszegi 2014; Kersten and Noronha 1999a), e.g. a negotiation dance graph

(Raiffa 1982), which emphasises the convergence of two negotiators by their actual utility values. In order to achieve this, preference information of both negotiation partners is considered. Other visualisation support only uses preference information of the focal negotiation party not to disclose own preferences to the negotiation partner, e.g. the history graph, which is shown in Figure 21.

The goal of such visualisation aids for multi-criteria decision making is to empower the decision maker with an understanding of the problem and possible solutions to be compared (Miettinen 2014). In the case of requirements negotiations, offers, which include issues and values, for which up-to-date preferences are available, can be visualised and assessed easily. However, visualisation of offers, whose preferences are outdated, or even for which a different agenda holds than is currently negotiated, is more complex. Several options to visualise such offers are to consider, e.g. to hide offers, which cannot be assessed by the current utility model, to assess outdated offers by their utility model at the time, or to assess only the utility of an offer's issues, which exist in the current agenda displaying the corresponding utility of the current preferences. While the first option would suppress displaying the concession making progress and the second option would be prone for misinterpreting the progress, the third option would disregard the progress at the time, however, represent the past offers' actual up-to-date benefit and their path. Which visualisation provides the most benefit for the negotiator could be studied in future research.

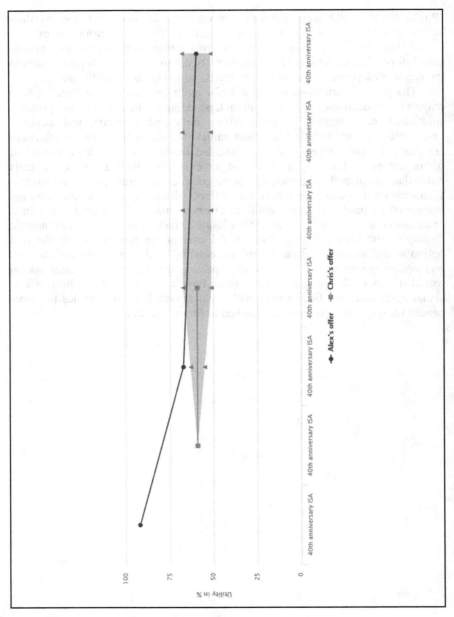

Figure 21: Exemplary history graph by Negoisst

References

Abbasgholizadeh Rahimi S, Jamshidi A, Ruiz A, Ait-kadi D (2016) A new dynamic integrated framework for surgical patients' prioritization considering risks and uncertainties. Decision Support Systems 88, pp 112–120

Almeida AT de, Wachowicz T (2017) Preference Analysis and Decision Support in Negotiations and Group Decisions. Group Decis Negot 26, pp 649–652

Aloysius JA, Davis FD, Wilson DD, Ross Taylor A, Kottemann JE (2006) User acceptance of multi-criteria decision support systems: The impact of preference elicitation techniques. European Journal of Operational Research 169, pp 273–285

AL-Ta'ani RH, Razali R (2013) Prioritizing Requirements in Agile Development: A Conceptual Framework. Procedia Technology 11, pp 733–739

Arnott D, Pervan G (2012) Design Science in Decision Support Systems Research: An Assessment using the Hevner, March, Park, and Ram Guidelines. Journal of the Association for Information Systems 13, pp 923–949

Arnott D, Pervan G (2014) A critical analysis of decision support systems research revisited: The rise of design science. J Inf Technol 29, pp 269–293

Aurum A, Wohlin C (2003) The fundamental nature of requirements engineering activities as a decision-making process. Information and Software Technology 45, pp 945–954

Ausubel LM, Cramton P, Deneckere RJ (2002) Bargaining with incomplete information. In: Handbook of Game Theory with Economic Applications Volume 3, vol 3. Elsevier, pp 1897–1945

Baskerville R, Pries-Heje J (2010) Explanatory Design Theory. Bus Inf Syst Eng 2, pp 271–282

Beck K, Beedle M, van Bennekum A, Cockburn A, Cunningham W, Fowler M, Grenning J, Highsmith J, Hunt A, Jeffries R, Kern J, Marick B, Martin RC, Mellor S, Schwaber K, Sutherland J, Thomas D (2001a) Manifesto for Agile Software Development. http://agilemanifesto.org/. Accessed 12 December 2016

Beck K, Beedle M, van Bennekum A, Cockburn A, Cunningham W, Fowler (2001b) Principles behind the Agile Manifesto. http://agilemanifesto.org/principles.html. Accessed 6 May 2017

Benítez J, Delgado-Galván X, Izquierdo J, Pérez-García R (2012) An approach to AHP decision in a dynamic context. Decision Support Systems 53, pp 499–506

Bergsmann J (2014) Requirements Engineering für die agile Softwareentwicklung: Methoden, Techniken und Strategien. dpunkt, Heidelberg

Bichler M, Kersten G, Strecker S (2003) Towards a Structured Design of Electronic Negotiations. Group Decision and Negotiation 12, pp 311–335

Boehm B, Kitapci H (2006) The WinWin Approach: Using a Requirements Negotiation Tool for Rationale Capture and Use. In: Dutoit AH, McCall R, Mistrík I, Paech B (eds) Rationale Management in Software Engineering. Springer, Dordrecht, Netherlands, pp 173–190

Boehm B, Grünbacher P, Briggs RO (2001) Developing groupware for requirements negotiation: lessons learned. IEEE Softw. 18, pp 46–55

Brans JP, Vincke P (1985) Note—A Preference Ranking Organisation Method. Management Science 31, pp 647–656

Brehm SS, Brehm JW (1981) Psychological reactance: A theory of freedom and control. Academic Press, New York

Brzostowski J, Wachowicz T (2014) NegoManage: A System for Supporting Bilateral Negotiations. Group Decis Negot 23, pp 463–496

Carroll JM (2000) Making use: Scenario-based design of human-computer interactions. MIT Press, Cambridge, Massachusetts, USA

Certa A, Enea M, Lupo T (2013) ELECTRE III to dynamically support the decision maker about the periodic replacements configurations for a multi-component system. Decision Support Systems 55, pp 126–134

Chen S-J, Hwang C-L (1992) Fuzzy multiple attribute decision making: Methods and applications. Lecture notes in economics and mathematical systems, ISBN 0075-8442, vol 375. Springer-Verlag, Berlin

Chen E, Vahidov R, Kersten GE (2005) Agent-supported negotiations in the e-marketplace. IJEB 3, pp 28–49

Clarke RJ, Kautz K (2014) What's in a user story: IS development methods as communication. In: Proceedings of the 23rd International Conference on Information Systems Development. University of Zagreb, Croatia, pp 356–364

Curhan JR, Neale MA, Ross L (2004) Dynamic valuation: Preference changes in the context of face-to-face negotiation. Journal of Experimental Social Psychology 40, pp 142–151

Dabholkar PA (1994) Incorporating Choice into an Attitudinal Framework: Analyzing Models of Mental Comparison Processes. J CONSUM RES 21, pp 100–118

Dahan E, Yee M, Hauser JR, Orlin J (2004) Conjoint Adaptive Ranking Database System (CARDS): AMA EXPLOR Award Winning presentation. http://www.anderson.ucla.edu/faculty/ely.dahan/content/EXPLOR_Award_Winner.ppt. Accessed 26 May 2017

Damian D, Lanubile F, Mallardo T (2008) On the Need for Mixed Media in Distributed Requirements Negotiations. IIEEE Trans. Software Eng. 34, pp 116–132

Danielson M, Ekenberg L (2016) The CAR Method for Using Preference Strength in Multi-criteria Decision Making. Group Decis Negot 25, pp 775–797

Davis FD, Bagozzi RP, Warshaw PR (1989) User Acceptance of Computer Technology: A Comparison of Two Theoretical Models. Management Science 35, pp 982–1003

DeSarbo WS, Fong DKH, Liechty J, Coupland JC (2005) Evolutionary preference/utility functions: A dynamic perspective. Psychometrika 70, pp 179–202

Eckert J, Schaaf R (2009) Verfahren zur Präferenzmessung – Eine Übersicht und Beurteilung existierender und möglicher neuer Self-Explicated-Verfahren. Journal für Betriebswirtschaft 59, pp 31–56

Elsler R, Schoop M (2012) Konzept eines Präferenzmodells basierend auf der GRIP Methodologie im Kontext elektronischer Verhandlungen. In: Mattfeld DC, Robra-Bissantz S (eds) Multikonferenz Wirtschaftsinformatik 2012: Tagungsband der MKWI 2012. Gito, Berlin, pp 1871–1884

Engin A, Vetschera R (2017) Information representation in decision making: The impact of cognitive style and depletion effects. Decision Support Systems 103, pp 94–103

Felfernig A, Zehentner C, Ninaus G, Grabner H, Maalej W, Pagano D, Weninger L, Reinfrank F (2012) Group Decision Support for Requirements Negotiation. In: Hutchison D, Kanade T, Kittler J, Kleinberg JM, Mattern F, Mitchell JC, Naor M, Nierstrasz O, Pandu Rangan C, Steffen B, Sudan M, Terzopoulos D, Tygar D, Vardi MY, Weikum G, Ardissono L, Kuflik T (eds) Advances in User Modeling. Springer Berlin Heidelberg, Berlin, Heidelberg, pp 105–116

Fernandes M (2016) Agenda negotiations in electronic negotiation support systems: An information systems perspective. Books on Demand, Norderstedt, Germany

Festinger L (1957) A theory of cognitive dissonance. Stanford University Press, Stanford, Calif.

Franch X, Carvallo JP (2002) A quality-model-based approach for describing and evaluating software packages. In: Proceedings: 9-13 September 2002, Essen, Germany. IEEE Computer Soc, Los Alamitos, Calif. [u.a.], pp 104–111

French S, Maule J, Papamichail N (2009) Decision behaviour, analysis and support. Cambridge University Press, Cambridge, United Kingdom

Fricker S, Grünbacher P (2008) Negotiation Constellations - Method Selection Framework for Requirements Negotiation. In: Paech B, Rolland C (eds) Proceedings Requirements Engineering: Foundation for Software Quality (REFSQ): 14th International Working Conference. Springer, Berlin Heidelberg, Germany, pp 37–51

Gerow JE, Ayyagari R, Thatcher JB, Roth PL (2013) Can we have fun @ work? The role of intrinsic motivation for utilitarian systems. Eur J Inf Syst 22, pp 360–380

Gettinger J, Koeszegi ST (2014) Far from Eye, Far from Heart: Analysis of Graphical Decision Aids in Electronic Negotiation Support. Group Decis Negot 23, pp 787–817

Gettinger J, Koeszegi ST, Schoop M (2012) Shall we dance? - The effect of information presentations on negotiation processes and outcomes. Decision Support Systems 53, pp 161–174

Górecka D, Roszkowska E, Wachowicz T (2016) The MARS Approach in the Verbal and Holistic Evaluation of the Negotiation Template. Group Decis Negot 25, pp 1097–1136

Greco S, Mousseau V, Słowiński R (2008) Ordinal regression revisited: Multiple criteria ranking using a set of additive value functions. European Journal of Operational Research 191, pp 416–436

Greco S, Mousseau V, Słowiński R (2014) Robust ordinal regression for value functions handling interacting criteria. European Journal of Operational Research 239, pp 711–730

Green PE (1984) Hybrid Models for Conjoint Analysis: An Expository Review. Journal of Marketing Research 21, pp 155

Green PE, Srinivasan V (1990) Conjoint Analysis in Marketing: New Developments with Implications for Research and Practice. Journal of Marketing 54, pp 3–19

Gregor S, Hevner AR (2013) Positioning and Presenting Design Science Research for Maximum Impact. MIS Quarterly 37, pp 337–355

Gregor S, Jones D (2007) The Anatomy of a Design Theory. Journal of the Association for Information Systems 8, pp 312–335

Grünbacher P, Seyff N (2005) Requirements Negotiation. In: Aurum A, Wohlin C (eds) Engineering and Managing Software Requirements. Springer, Berlin Heidelberg, Germany, pp 143–162

Grünbacher P, Köszegi S, Biffl S (2006) Stakeholder Value Proposition Elicitation and Reconsiliation. In: Biffl S, Aurum A, Boehm B, Erdogmus H, Grünbacher P (eds) Value based software engineering. Springer, Berlin, Heidelberg [u.a.], pp 133–154

Guo Y, Müller JP, Weinhardt C (2003) Learning User Preferences for Multi-attribute Negotiation: An Evolutionary Approach. In: Mařík V, Pěchouček M, Müller J (eds) Multi-Agent Systems and Applications III. Springer Berlin Heidelberg, pp 303–313

Gustafsson A, Herrmann A, Huber F (eds) (2007) Conjoint Measurement: Methods and Applications, 4th ed. Springer, Berlin, New York, vii, 373 p.

Hansen S, Lyytinen K, Kharabe A (2015) A Tale of Requirements Computation in Two Projects: A Distributed Cognition View. In: ICIS 2015 Proceedings, paper 12

Helbig M, Deb K, Engelbrecht A (2016) Key challenges and future directions of dynamic multi-objective optimisation. In: 2016 IEEE Congress on Evolutionary Computation (CEC), Vancouver, BC, Canada, pp 1256–1261

Herbst U, Schwarz S (2011) How Valid Is Negotiation Research Based on Student Sample Groups?: New Insights into a Long-Standing Controversy. Negotiation Journal 27, pp 147–170

Herbst U, Voeth M (2015) An Empirical Comparison of Computer-Based Conjoint Variants in Multi-Attributive Purchase Decisions. In: Robinson L (ed) Proceedings of the 2008 Academy of Marketing Science (AMS) Annual Conference. Springer, Cham, Switzerland, p 240

Herzwurm G, Schoop M, Reiser A, Krams B (2012) E-requirements negotiation: Electronic negotiations in the distributed software development. In: Mattfeld DC, Robra-Bissantz S (eds) Multikonferenz Wirtschaftsinformatik 2012: Tagungsband der MKWI 2012. Gito, Berlin, pp 1859–1870

Hevner A, Chatterjee S (2010) Design Research in Information Systems: Theory and Practice. Integrated Series in Information Systems, vol 22. Springer, New York Dordrecht Heidelberg London

Hevner AR (2007) A Three Cycle View of Design Science Research. Scandinavian Journal of Information Systems 19, article 4

Hevner AR, March ST, Park J, Ram S (2004) Design science in information systems research. MIS Q 28, pp 75–105

Hull E, Jackson K, Dick J (2011) Requirements engineering. Springer, London, United Kingdom

Hwang C-L, Lai Y-J, Liu T-Y (1993) A new approach for multiple objective decision making. Computers & Operations Research 20, pp 889–899

In H, Olson D (2004) Requirements Negotiation Using Multi-Criteria Preference Analysis. Journal of Computer Science 10, pp 306–325

Inayat I, Salim SS, Marczak S, Daneva M, Shamshirband S (2015) A systematic literature review on agile requirements engineering practices and challenges. Computers in Human Behavior 51, pp 915–929

Institute of Electrical and Electronics Engineers (1990) IEEE standard glossary of software engineering terminology: 610.12-1990. Institute of Electrical and Electronics Engineers, New York

Jacquet-Lagreze E, Siskos J (1982) Assessing a set of additive utility functions for multicriteria decision-making, the UTA method. European Journal of Operational Research 10, pp 151–164

Jacquet-Lagrèze E, Siskos Y (2001) Preference disaggregation: 20 years of MCDA experience. European Journal of Operational Research 130, pp 233–245

Jarke M, Lyytinen K (2015) Editorial: "Complexity of Systems Evolution: Requirements Engineering Perspective". ACM Trans. Manage. Inf. Syst. 5, article 11

Johnson RM (1987) Adaptive Conjoint Analysis. In: Sawtooth Software Conference Proceedings. Sawtooth Software, Ketchum, ID, pp 253–265

Kadziński M, Greco S, Słowiński R (2012) Selection of a representative value function in robust multiple criteria ranking and choice. European Journal of Operational Research 217, pp 541–553

Keeney RL, Raiffa H (1976) Decisions with multiple objectives: Preferences and value tradeoffs. Wiley series in probability and mathematical statistics. Wiley, New York, USA

Kersten G, Lai H (2010) Electronic Negotiations: Foundations, Systems, and Processes. In: Kilgour DM, Eden C (eds) Handbook of Group Decision and Negotiation, vol 4. Springer, Dordrecht, Netherlands, pp 361–392

Kersten G, Noronha S (1999a) Negotiation via the World Wide Web: A Cross-cultural Study of Decision Making. Group Decis Negot 8, pp 251–279

Kersten G, Roszkowska E, Wachowicz T (2017) The Heuristics and Biases in Using the Negotiation Support Systems. In: Schoop M, Kilgour DM (eds) Group Decision and Negotiation. A Socio-Technical Perspective: 17th International Conference, GDN 2017, Stuttgart, Germany, August 14-18, 2017, Proceedings. Springer International Publishing, Cham, pp 215–228

Kersten GE, Szpakowicz S, Koperczak Z (1990) Modelling of decision making for discrete processes in dynamic environments. Computers & Mathematics with Applications 20, pp 29–43

Kersten GE, Noronha SJ (1999b) WWW-based negotiation support: Design, implementation, and use. Decision Support Systems 25, pp 135–154

Köhne F, Schoop M, Staskiewicz D (2005) An Empirical Investigation of the Acceptance of Electronic Negotiation Support System Features. In: Bartmann D, Rajola F, Kallinikos J, Avison D, Winter R, Ein-Dor P, Becker J, Bodendorf F, Weinhardt C (eds) 13th European Conference on Information Systems: Proceedings, Regensburg, Germany, paper 158

Kukreja N (2012) Winbook: A social networking based framework for collaborative requirements elicitation and WinWin negotiations. In: 34th International Conference on Software Engineering (ICSE), pp 1610–1612

Kukreja N, Boehm B (2013) Integrating Collaborative Requirements Negotiation and Prioritization Processes: A Match Made in Heaven. In: International Conference on Software and System Process (ICSSP), pp 141–145

Lai S-K (1995) A preference-based interpretation of AHP. Omega 23, pp 453–462

Lai H, Lin H-C, Lin W-J (2007) NeGoGo: ANeGo and SynNeGo. In: Kersten GE, Rios J, Chen E (eds) Group decision and negotiation 2007. InterNeg Research Center, Montreal, pp 75–81

Lai H, Lin W-J, Kersten GE (2010) The importance of language familiarity in global business e-negotiation. Electronic Commerce Research and Applications 9, pp 537–548

Lenz A (2018) Supporting Decisions in Requirements Negotiations Dynamically. In: Gesellschaft für Informatik (ed) Softwaretechnik-Trends, pp 39–40

Lenz A (2019) Designing Dynamic Decision Support for Electronic Requirements Negotiations. In: Ludwig T, Pipek V (eds) 14th International Conference on Wirtschaftsinformatik: Tagungsband, pp 1160–1174

Lenz A, Schoop M (2017) Decision Problems in Requirements Negotiations – Identifying the Underlying Structures. In: Schoop M, Kilgour DM (eds) Group Decision and Negotiation. A Socio-Technical Perspective: 17th International Conference, GDN 2017, Stuttgart, Germany, August 14-18, 2017, Proceedings. Springer International Publishing, Cham, pp 120–131

Lenz A, Schoop M (2019) Assessment of Multi-Criteria Preference Measurement Methods for a Dynamic Environment. In: Proceedings of the 52nd Hawaii International Conference on System Sciences, pp 1803–1812

Lenz A, Schoop M, Herzwurm G (2015) Requirements Analysis as a Negotiation Process. In: Kaminski B, Kersten G, Szufel P, Jakubczyk M, Wachowicz T (eds) The 15th International Conference on Group Decision & Negotiation letters. Warsaw School of Economics Press, Warsaw, Poland, pp 303–309

Lenz A, Schoop M, Herzwurm G (2016) Electronic Requirements Negotiation - A Literature Survey on the State-of-the-Art. In: UK Academy for Information Systems Conference (ed) Proceedings of UKAIS 2016 (Oxford), paper 23

Li G, Kou G, Peng Y (2015) DYNAMIC FUZZY MULTIPLE CRITERIA DECISION MAKING FOR PERFORMANCE EVALUATION. Technological and Economic Development of Economy 21, pp 705–719

Liechty JC, Fong DKH, DeSarbo WS (2005) Dynamic Models Incorporating Individual Heterogeneity: Utility Evolution in Conjoint Analysis. Marketing Science 24, pp 285–293

Lim L-H, Benbasat I (1992) A Theoretical Perspective of Negotiation Support Systems. Journal of Management Information Systems 9, pp 27–44

Luce RD, Raiffa H (1957) Games and Decisions: Introduction and Critical Survey. John Wiley & Sons, Inc., New York, NY, USA

Martin N, Gregor S (2005) Requirements Engineering: A Case of Developing and Managing Quality Software Systems in the Public Sector. In: Aurum A, Wohlin C (eds) Engineering and Managing Software Requirements. Springer, Berlin Heidelberg, Germany, pp 353–372

Matzner M, von Hoffen M, Heide T, Plenter F, Chasin F (2015) A Method for Measuring User Preferences in Information Systems Design Choices. In: ECIS 2015 Completed Research Papers, Paper 131

Meißner M, Decker R, Adam N (2011) Ein empirischer Validitätsvergleich zwischen Adaptive Self-Explicated Approach (ASE), Pairwise Comparison-based Preference Measurement (PCPM) und Adaptive Conjoint Analysis (ACA). Z Betriebswirtsch 81, pp 423–446

Miettinen K (2014) Survey of methods to visualize alternatives in multiple criteria decision making problems. OR Spektrum 36, pp 3–37

Moe NB, Aurum A, Dybå T (2012) Challenges of shared decision-making: A multiple case study of agile software development. Information and Software Technology 54, pp 853–865

Mu K, Liu W, Jin Z, Hong J, Bell D (2011) Managing Software Requirements Changes Based on Negotiation-Style Revision. Journal of Computer Science and Technology 26, pp 890–907

Mumpower JL (1991) The Judgment Policies of Negotiators and the Structure of Negotiation Problems. Management Science 37, pp 1304–1324

Nebro AJ, Ruiz AB, Barba-González C, García-Nieto J, Luque M, Aldana-Montes JF (2018) InDM2: Interactive Dynamic Multi-Objective Decision Making Using Evolutionary Algorithms. Swarm and Evolutionary Computation 40, pp 184–195

Netzer O, Srinivasan V (2011) Adaptive Self-Explication of Multiattribute Preferences. Journal of Marketing Research 48, pp 140–156

Netzer O, Toubia O, Bradlow ET, Dahan E, Evgeniou T, Feinberg FM, Feit EM, Hui SK, Johnson J, Liechty JC, Orlin JB, Rao VR (2008) Beyond conjoint analysis: Advances in preference measurement. Mark Lett 19, pp 337–354

Ngo-The A, Ruhe G (2005) Decision Support in Requirements Engineering. In: Aurum A, Wohlin C (eds) Engineering and Managing Software Requirements. Springer, Berlin Heidelberg, Germany, pp 267–286

Nunnally JC, Bernstein IH (1994) Psychometric theory. McGraw-Hill series in psychology. McGraw-Hill, New York

Pendergast WR (1990) Managing the negotiation agenda. Negotiation Journal 6, pp 135–145

Pohl K (2010) Requirements engineering: Fundamentals, principles, and techniques. Springer, Heidelberg, New York

Price J, Cybulski J (2006) The Importance of IS Stakeholder Perspectives and Perceptions to Requirements Negotiation. In: Zowghi D, Nguyen L, Swatman P (eds) Proceedings of the 11th Australian Workshop on Requirements Engineering. University of South Australia, Adelaide, Australia

Raiffa H (1982) The art and science of negotiation. Belknap Press of Harvard University Press, Cambridge, Massachusetts, USA

Raiffa H, Richardson J, Metcalfe D (2002) Negotiation analysis: The science and art of collaborative decision making. Belknap Press of Harvard University Press, Cambridge, Massachusetts, USA

Ramesh B, Cao L, Baskerville R (2010) Agile requirements engineering practices and challenges: An empirical study. Information Systems Journal 20, pp 449–480

Reiser A (2013) Entscheidungsunterstützung in elektronischen Verhandlungen: Eine Analyse unter besonderer Berücksichtigung von unvollständigen Informationen. Springer, Wiesbaden, Germany

Reiser A, Schoop M (2012) Considering Incomplete Information in Negotiation Support Systems. In: Almeida ATd, Morais DC, Daher SdFD (eds) Group Decision and Negotiation 2012 Proceedings, Editora Universitária UFPE, pp 112–113

Reiser A, Krams B, Schoop M (2012) Requirements Negotiation in Consideration of Dynamics and Interactivity. In: Proceedings of the REFSQ 2012 Workshops and the Conference Related Empirical Study, Empirical Fair and Doctoral Symposium, ICB Research Report No. 52, Duisburg-Essen, Germany, pp 163–174

Renzel D, Behrendt M, Klamma R, Jarke M (2013) Requirements Bazaar: Social Requirements Engineering for Community-Driven Innovation. In: 21st IEEE International Requirements Engineering Conference Proceedings, pp 326–327

Roszkowska E, Wachowicz T (2015a) Application of fuzzy TOPSIS to scoring the negotiation offers in ill-structured negotiation problems. European Journal of Operational Research 242, pp 920–932

Roszkowska E, Wachowicz T (2015b) Inaccuracy in Defining Preferences by the Electronic Negotiation System Users. In: Kamiński B, Kersten GE, Szapiro T (eds) Outlooks and Insights on Group Decision and Negotiation: 15th International Conference, GDN 2015, Warsaw, Poland, June 22-26, 2015, Proceedings. Springer International Publishing, Cham, pp 131–143

Roy B (1990) The Outranking Approach and the Foundations of Electre Methods. In: Bana e Costa, Carlos A. (ed) Readings in Multiple Criteria Decision Aid. Springer Berlin Heidelberg, pp 155–183

Ruhe G, Eberlein A, Pfahl D (2002) Quantitative WinWin – A New Method for Decision Support in Requirements Negotiation. In: Proceedings of the 14th International Conference on Software Engineering and Knowledge Engineering (SEKE), pp 159–166

Saaty TL (1990) How to make a decision: The analytic hierarchy process. European Journal of Operational Research 48, pp 9–26

Sawtooth Software, Inc. (2007) ACA System for Adaptive Conjoint Analysis. The ACA/Web v6.0. Technical Paper. https://www.sawtoothsoftware.com/support/technical-papers/aca-related-papers/aca-technical-paper-2007. Accessed 9 March 2017

Schlereth C, Eckert C, Schaaf R, Skiera B (2014) Measurement of preferences with self-explicated approaches: A classification and merge of trade-off- and non-trade-off-based evaluation types. European Journal of Operational Research 238, pp 185–198

Scholz SW, Meissner M, Decker R (2010) Measuring Consumer Preferences for Complex Products: A Compositional Approach Based on Paired Comparisons. Journal of Marketing Research 47, pp 685–698

Schoop M (2005) A Language-Action Approach to Electronic Negotiations. Systems, Signs & Actions 1, pp 62–79

Schoop M (2010) Support of Complex Electronic Negotiations. In: Kilgour DM, Eden C (eds) Handbook of Group Decision and Negotiation, vol 4. Springer, Dordrecht, Netherlands, pp 409–423

Schoop M, Jertila A, List T (2003) Negoisst: A Negotiation Support System for Electronic Business-to-Business Negotiations in E-Commerce. Data & Knowledge Engineering 47, pp 371–401

Schoop M, Amelsvoort M, Gettinger J, Koerner M, Koeszegi S, Wijst P (2014) The Interplay of Communication and Decisions in Electronic Negotiations: Communicative Decisions or Decisive Communication? Group Decis Negot 23, pp 167–192

Simon HA (1955) A Behavioral Model of Rational Choice. The Quarterly Journal of Economics 69, pp 99–118

Simons T, Tripp TM (2010) The Negotiation Checklist. In: Lewicki RJ, Saunders DM, Barry B (eds) Negotiation: Readings, exercises, and cases, 6th ed. McGraw-Hill Higher Education, New York, pp 34–47

Sommerville I (2012) Software Engineering. Pearson Studium - IT. Pearson, München

Spliet R, Tervonen T (2014) Preference inference with general additive value models and holistic pair-wise statements. European Journal of Operational Research 232, pp 607–612

Srinivasan V, Park CS (1997) Surprising Robustness of the Self-Explicated Approach to Customer Preference Structure Measurement. Journal of Marketing Research 34, pp 286

Thakurta R (2017) Understanding requirement prioritization artifacts: A systematic mapping study. Requirements Eng 22, pp 491–526

Thiessen EM, Soberg A (2003) SmartSettle Described with the Montreal Taxonomy. Group Decis Negot 12, pp 165–170

Thompson LL (2012) The mind and heart of the negotiator. Pearson Education Inc, Boston, Massachusetts, USA

Toubia O, Simester DI, Hauser JR, Dahan E (2003) Fast Polyhedral Adaptive Conjoint Estimation. Marketing Science 22, pp 273–303

van de Walle B, Campbell C, Deek FP (2007) The Impact of Task Structure and Negotiation Sequence on Distributed Requirements Negotiation Activity, Conflict, and Satisfaction. In: Proceedings of the 19th International Conference on Advanced information systems engineering (CAiSE), pp 381–394

Vetschera R (2006) Preference-Based Decision Support in Software Engineering. In: Biffl S, Aurum A, Boehm B, Erdogmus H, Grünbacher P (eds) Value based software engineering. Springer, Berlin, Heidelberg [u.a.]

Vetschera R (2007) Preference structures and negotiator behavior in electronic negotiations. Decision Support Systems 44, pp 135–146

Vetschera R (2016) Concessions Dynamics in Electronic Negotiations: A Cross-Lagged Regression Analysis. Group Decis Negot 25, pp 245–265

Vetschera R, Filzmoser M (2012) Standardized interpolated path analysis of offer processes in e-negotiations. In: Proceedings of the 14th Annual International Conference on Electronic Commerce. ACM, Singapore, Singapore, pp 134–140

Vetschera R, Kersten G, Koeszegi S (2006) User Assessment of Internet-Based Negotiation Support Systems: An Exploratory Study. Journal of Organizational Computing and Electronic Commerce 16, pp 123–148

Vlaanderen K, Jansen S, Brinkkemper S, Jaspers E (2011) The agile requirements refinery: Applying SCRUM principles to software product management. Information and Software Technology 53, pp 58–70

Voeth M (2000) Nutzenmessung in der Kaufverhaltensforschung: Die Hierarchische Individualisierte Limit Conjoint-Analyse (HILCA). Deutscher Universitätsverlag, Wiesbaden, Germany

Voeth M, Herbst U, Tobies I (2007) Customer Insights on Industrial Markets – A New Method to Measure Complex Preferences. In: Proceedings of the IMP Group Conference, Manchester, United Kingdom

Yuan YMGD (2003) Online Negotiation in Electronic Commerce. International Journal of Management Theory and Practices 4, pp 39–48

Zhang Y, Ying J, Bai J, Zhang J (2013) A Negotiation Framework for Managing the Requirements Changes. Cybernetics and Information Technologies 13, pp 75–87

Appendix

A1   Case Study Information Including Preferences for Initial Preference Elicitation

General Information

The Institute for Teaching and Learning (ITL) is a national organisation, which provides educational software for schools, universities, and companies. Originally it was founded as a governmental institution in 2000. The ITL became one of the biggest suppliers for educational software within the country, not least because of governmental subsidies.

ITL's roots lie in the software for national public education. However, it grew fast and expanded to educational context of other countries. Within the first seven years and with a growing network of contacts, the strategy of ITL changed to becoming a global vendor for educational software. Becoming a global software supplier, ITL tries to expand to sell learning software to companies. ITL now supplies profit as well as non-profit organisations. Nowadays, with customers in 28 countries, ITL is one of the world's largest suppliers for educational software.

The General Student Committee (GeSCo) is a student organisation, which represents the students' interests, especially manages funds in the students' best interests. For the upcoming financing period, GeSCo explores possible projects. One of them is the project of introducing an Audience Response System (ARS). ARSs aim to support the interaction between presenter and the audience in lectures or presentations with numerous participants. The use of such systems is mostly driven by didactic concepts, thus, ARSs are part of e-learning. ARSs allow large groups to vote on certain aspects or to answer questions during a presentation. Most systems combine the concept of bring your own device, so involve the audience's devices, with a presentation software, which provides the functionality.

The university already maintains a learning management system (LMS) developed by GeSCo. An LMS is a software application for the administration, documentation, tracking, reporting and delivery of educational courses. LMSs help the lecturer deliver material to the students, administer assignments, and track student progress. Ilias is an example for an LMS.

Hence, GeSCo has asked ITL, if they also sell ARSs. ITL does not distribute ARSs yet, however, ITL has recognised the demand of ARSs in educational context independently of GeSCo's inquiry and first concepts of the development

A. Lenz, *Dynamic Decision Support for Electronic Requirements Negotiations*, https://doi.org/10.1007/978-3-658-31175-9

exist. ITL is still looking for representative customers, whose requirements they can implement in their future ARS to build a product, which is generic enough to satisfy other potential customers' needs, to take root in the ARS business. GeS-Co and ITL have decided to conduct informal preliminary discussions about a cooperation, in which ITL will develop an ARS based on GeSCo's requirements.

These first discussions have already been conducted so far. The aim is to use the ARS in large courses. There will be two roles, "lecturer" and "student". Lecturers can manage courses and use the ARS during lectures for surveys or brainstorming, the students can register to courses, post questions or comments and answer a survey or a brainstorming.

However, some requirements and their implementation are yet unclear. Unclear issues are standalone or integration, registration, product name, interfaces, brainstorming function, concurrent users, and device support. You are Toni Bauer, member of GeSCo and part of the negotiation team. Before you can negotiate the issues to resolve, first the preferences for the single issues and their possible values must be elicited. You already know, that for the last unclear issue, device support, the possible values are not settled yet, so you cannot elicit your preferences for this issue. However, you must elicit preferences for the known issues and values, because negotiations will start soon. You will meet with ITL on Friday to discuss your co-operation, however, it is unclear, if all relevant information for the last issue will be cleared in this meeting.

Private information about the issues

Standalone software or component of the LMS: There are two possible options to implement the ARS. The ARS can either be implemented as a standalone software or it can be integrated as a component of the LMS the university already maintains. Your preferred option is to implement it as an integrated component.

Registration: Obviously, the ARS requires user authentication. Registration of lecturers and students must be possible. One option of this issue is to use the lecturers' and students' existing university accounts. This is a good option, because no-one has to create an extra account for the ARS and no new administration and support processes are required. However, an open question is how to handle guest lecturers or students of cooperative study programmes who do not have a university account. So, the second option, which is your best case, is to use existing university accounts and to provide registration processes for additional accounts. The third option is to use ITL accounts. This means, that users would have to register themselves at ITL. An advantage of this solution is that everybody can create an account, but this is a major disadvantage at the same time, because lecturers and students are forced to create an extra account at ITL.

Product name: Since GeSCo got financial support, the project must be a success and gain good reputation by the students. So, the ARS needs a good name, which needs to be prominently put on every page. There are the following options: The ARS is named by GeSCo, the ARS is named by ITL, or there will be two names, one for the software product (by ITL) and one for the instantiation of the software (by GeSCo).

Interfaces: The minimum requirement is to import slides into the ARS to show them during the lecture. However, an automated import of course slides of the LMS is preferred. Moreover, it should be possible, to extract students' behaviour data anonymously out of the ARS.

Brainstorming function: The lecturer creates a brainstorming for a single lecture. For this, the lecturer provides a question and starts the brainstorming during the lecture. Students can participate in the brainstorming afterwards by posting ideas. The lecturer can sort, delete, hide, or edit ideas. An option is that the lecturer can transform the brainstorming results into a survey. This will be a great benefit for the ARS. However, you noticed, that ITL is sceptical about this.

Concurrent users: GeSCo plans with five concurrent large lectures of 500 students on average. So, the ARS should provide at least 2.500 users concurrent access during the lectures in the worst case. The university has approximately 10.000 students. However, it is estimated that about 40 % will use the ARS concurrently at maximum. So, 4.000 concurrent accesses should be possible in the best case.

Supported devices: This issue deals with the question, which devices to support. Will there be a version for backend access, a smartphone version or a tablet version. If the device question is clarified, which browser will be supported? Or will there be an app for smartphones and tablets? If so, will the app be available for each smartphone? Since these questions are not clarified yet, this issue is postponed to the meeting of GeSCo and ITL scheduled on Friday.

After having discussed these issues previously with other GeSCo members, you came up with the following preferences:

Issue	Importance	Value	Preference
Standalone or integration	36 %	Standalone	0
		Integration	100
Registration	16 %	University accounts	80
		University accounts and guest accounts	100
		ITL accounts	0
Product name	12 %	GeSCo	100
		ITL	0
		Two names	40
Interfaces	8 %	Manual slides import	0
		Automated slides import	70
		Manual slides import and data export	30
		Automated slides import and data export	100
Brainstorming	8 %	Transformation into survey	100
		No transformation	0
Concurrent users	20 %	2.500	0
		4.000	100
Supported devices	???	???	???

A2   Case Study Information Including Preferences after Agenda Change for Preference Adjustment

Private information

You took part in today's meeting of GeSCo with ITL. You could clarify the issue "Supported devices" and generate options to resolve it. You agreed on a backend version and a smartphone version. Regarding the smartphone version, two possible options are to provide, either a native app for the two most popular phones, StarPhone and MarcPhone, or a WebApp. You prefer native apps to ensure offline functionality. Although, students must connect to WiFi during the lectures to participate, they can use the app offline, when the live-features are not required.

The preference information for the new issue "Supported devices" as well as the relative importance of the new issue are shown below:

Issue	Value	Preference
Supported devices	App for StarPhones and MarcPhones	100
	WebApp	0

Issue	Previous importance	New importance
Standalone or integration	36 %	27 %
Registration	16 %	12 %
Product name	12 %	9 %
Interfaces	8 %	6 %
Brainstorming	8 %	6 %
Concurrent users	20 %	15 %
Supported devices		25 %

A3   Factor Loadings after Rotation

Table 13:   Factor loadings after rotation

	1	2	3	4	5
The outcome of the preference adjustment reflects my actual preferences perfectly.	.907				
I could not ask for a more accurate result of the preference adjustment (in task 2).	.890				
Overall, my final elicited preferences are accurate.	.833				
In comparison to the actual preferences, my final preferences are very accurate.	.819				
Please note your perception of the accuracy of the preferences resulting from your use of the preference adjustment.	.726				
Overall I have confidence in negotiating in English.		.930			
I consider that I can negotiate in English fluently.		.891			
I consider that I have the ability to negotiate in English.		.882			
I consider it easy to negotiate in English.		.881			
The preference adjustment (task 2) was fun.			.968		
The preference adjustment (task 2) was entertaining.			.949		
The preference adjustment (task 2) was enjoyable.			.943		
The preference adjustment in task 2 was slow.				.891	
The preference adjustment in task 2 took a long time.				.870	
Compared to task 1, did the preference adjustment in task 2 take less time or more time?					.841
Compared to task 1, was the preference adjustment in task 2 slower or faster?				.389	.739

A4   Reliability Measures

Table 14:   Realibility measures

	Negotiation experience	Perceived accuracy	Perceived duration absolute	Perceived duration relative	Fun
Arithmetic mean	4.58	5.90	5.74	5.77	4.01
SD	1.32	0.97	1.17	1.00	1.55
Cronbach's α	.929	.897	.810	.465	.964
Composite reliability	.942	.921	.873	.659	.968
AVE	.803	.701	.775	.627	.909

Printed in the United States
By Bookmasters